Sales promotion and direct marketing law:
A practical guide

To Gaenor,
for her enormous support on this
and on everything else

Sales promotion and direct marketing law:
A practical guide

Fifth edition

Philip Circus MA, MPhil, DCA, FISP, Barrister
Director of Legal Affairs, Institute of Sales Promotion
Partner, Lawmark, the Marketing Law Advisory Service
Legal Adviser, British Promotional Merchandise Association
Regulatory Affairs Consultant, Internet Advertising Bureau

Tottel
publishing

Published by
Tottel Publishing Ltd
Maxwelton House
41–43 Boltro Road
Haywards Heath
West Sussex
RH16 1BJ

ISBN 978 1 84592 456 0
© Tottel Publishing Ltd 2007
Formerly published by LexisNexis Butterworths
Fifth edition published by Tottel Publishing Ltd 2007
Reprinted 2008 (twice)

British Library Cataloguing-in-Publication Data
A catalogue record for this book is available from the British Library

Typeset by Laserwords Pvt. Ltd., Chennai, India
Printed and bound in Great Britain by
Athenæum Press Limited, Gateshead, Tyne & Wear

PREFACE

One of the advantages of the law in relation to sales promotion and direct marketing has been in the past that it changed relatively infrequently and then only at the margins. Not so, as I write this at the beginning of 2007.

It is no exaggeration to say that we are experiencing the most significant change to the legal framework affecting promotional marketing I have known in 30 years. The main reason is the implementation from September 2007 of the Gambling Act—a piece of legislation which will re-cast the legal framework for prize promotions. We fully consider the implications in Chapter 4.

Further major developments are in train, particularly the implementation of the EU Unfair Commercial Practices Directive. However, we cannot cover the subject comprehensively in this edition because, at the time of writing, the detail of the necessary implementing legislation is not known.

Many people have helped me produce this 5th edition, particularly in giving me permission to reproduce the various documents in the Appendices. Samantha Hambury of the DMA was particularly helpful in keeping me up to speed on the various roles which the DMA plays in the framework of regulation. And, Roger Wisbey, Secretary of CAP, made a significant contribution to the description of the self-regulatory controls. My thanks to all of them.

I must express special thanks to the ISP whose support over the years has been crucially important to the success of this publication.

Finally my thanks go to my wife, Gaenor, who has the patience of a saint and has done the real work by preparing all of the manuscript for the publisher.

Philip Circus
West Chiltington, West Sussex
May 2007

ABOUT THE AUTHOR

The name Philip Circus has been closely associated with the legal side of marketing for 30 years—an involvement that has combined legal work in a number of major marketing trade associations with consultancy work for individual clients.

Educated at the Universities of London and Southampton and the College of Law, Philip Circus was called to the Bar by the Inner Temple in 1975. He has two Masters degrees, as well as the Diploma in Consumer Affairs of the Institute of Trading Standards—for which he won the Joe Routledge prize—and a Diploma in European Community Law from King's College, London. He also holds the Diploma of the Institute of Sales Promotion and was made a Fellow of the Institute in 2001 for 'outstanding services to the sales promotion industry'. He is also a Fellow of the British Promotional Merchandise Association and was awarded their Sword of Honour for services to the industry.

Philip Circus has held numerous positions relating to advertising and marketing, including Chairman of the CBI's Consumer Affairs Committee and membership of the Government's Working Parties on prices, credit and environmental labelling. He has been a member of the National Consumer Council, a Board member of the Mail Order Protection Scheme, a member of the ITC's Advertising Advisory Committee and a member of the Committee of Advertising Practice (CAP) since 1977—being Chairman of its Sales Promotion and Direct Response Panel.

He jointly founded the Advertising Law Group, which is the group of specialist legal practitioners in advertising and marketing law.

CONTENTS

INTRODUCTION TO THE LEGAL AND SELF-REGULATORY CONTROLS ON SALES PROMOTION AND DIRECT MARKETING

Legal controls

Question: What do we mean by 'sales promotion'?

Answer: Definitions of the various marketing disciplines are many. Certainly, to the author's knowledge the term 'sales promotion' is not defined in law, although there are definitions of 'advertisement'—definitions which sometimes include sales promotion and direct marketing. The Institute of Sales Promotion (ISP) defines sales promotion in the following terms:

> 'A marketing initiative, the purpose of which is to create a call to action that has a direct impact on the behaviour of the brand's target audience by offering a demonstrable benefit that is not necessarily tangible.'

However, for most purposes an everyday working definition would be 'temporary added value'.

Question: What do we mean by 'direct marketing'?

Answer: Section 11(3) of the Data Protection Act 1998 defines direct marketing as ' ... the communication (by whatever means) of any advertising or marketing material which is directed to particular individuals.'

Question: What do we mean by 'sales promotion law'?

Answer: People talk about sales promotion law as if it is a dedicated body of law in its own right. However, this is not so. It is doubtful whether the Parliamentary Counsel, the drafters of legislation, have even heard of the term 'sales promotion', let alone understood what it is and how it operates. Accordingly, when we talk of 'sales promotion law' what we mean is that collection of laws which has an incidental effect on sales promotion. Only the Trading Stamps Act 1964 was designed specifically to control a sales promotion technique and that legislation has now been repealed.

Question: What do we mean by 'direct marketing law'?

Answer: The answer is broadly the same as for the previous question. Of course, there is a major overlap between sales promotion law and direct marketing law—hence the combination of both in this book. Having said that, there are some laws that particularly come under one heading or the other, as we shall see later on.

Question: When we talk about 'law', what do we mean?

Answer: The law can be sub-divided into a number of categories, and these we consider in subsequent questions. One significant characteristic of the law is its comprehensiveness of application—unlike self-regulation, for example, which would normally only apply to members of an association. The main distinction within the law is between civil law and criminal law.

Civil law

Question: What is civil law?

Answer: Civil law is designed to assist individuals in enforcing what are essentially individual rights, for example, trespass, defamation and breach of contract. The point is that society as a whole is not involved, since the object of civil law is compensation for individual wrong rather than punishment.

Question: What courts are relevant to civil law matters?

Answer: Minor matters are dealt with by the county courts, and within the county courts there is provision for what are termed 'small claims'—invariably those consumer complaints which, although they raise important issues, nevertheless relate to relatively small sums of money. Cases can go to arbitration within the county court system and this does much to overcome some of the fear that people have of litigation.

More serious matters are dealt with at the High Court. Avenues of appeal lie to the Court of Appeal (Civil Division) and the House of Lords.

Criminal law

Question: What, then, is the purpose of the criminal law?

Answer: Criminal law deals with those wrongs which are considered to be more than just a question of individual rights. Accordingly, the State in its various guises, is the initiator of the action and the objective is not compensation but rather punishment and the suppression of crime. Having said that, the criminal courts can make use of the Powers of Criminal Courts (Sentencing) Act 2000 to award compensation to those who have suffered loss as a result of crime.

Question: Who enforces the criminal law that is relevant to sales promotion?

Answer: Most consumer protection law is enforced by trading standards officers who are local government employees. Such areas as consumer credit and the law on price indications are enforced by trading standards departments. An element of co-ordination of policy amongst the many trading standards departments is achieved through the Local Authorities Coordinators of Regulatory Services (LACORS) The Gambling Commission is responsible for enforcing the law relating to lotteries and competitions, and the Police are responsible for enforcing the law relating to bribery and corruption.

Question: What courts are relevant to the enforcement of the criminal law?

Answer: Most criminal cases are dealt with in the magistrates' courts. Some are tried there because they are called 'summary offences', which can only be dealt with by magistrates. Many more cases are dealt with there by the choice of the defendants. This is because defendants often have a choice of trial by magistrates or trial by jury at the Crown Court. Rarely do defendants choose the latter because of the time, expense and potentially greater sentence that can be awarded against them. Appeal from a decision of the magistrates can go either to the Crown Court or, on a point of law, to the Divisional Court. Further appeals are possible to the Court of Appeal (Criminal Division) and the House of Lords.

Question: People sometimes talk about 'case law' and sometimes about 'statute law'. What's the difference?

Answer: Unlike many continental countries, the basis of English law has been the decisions of the judges over the centuries in making precedents which are followed in later cases. These case decisions may involve the development of the common law, ie that part of the law which is based originally on the common unwritten customs of the country. Large parts of the law, both criminal and civil, are rooted in the common law. For example, although the law establishes the penalties for murder, the definition of murder is laid down by the common law and not by an Act of Parliament.

Case law may also throw light on the interpretation of statutes. By statute law, we mean the law which has emanated from Parliament through either Acts of Parliament or through statutory instruments (SIs), which are made by ministers under the authority given to them by Acts of Parliament. Statute law is increasingly important, particularly because the doctrine of judicial precedent means that decisions of judges are binding unless overruled by a higher court. As society has developed and as changes have taken place, Parliament has been seen as a far quicker way of changing the law than leaving changes to the judges. However, that does not mean that individual case decisions are not important. As we look at particular areas of sales promotion law we shall note some highly crucial court decisions.

Codes of practice

Question: What are codes of practice?

Answer: Codes of practice are very popular these days and there are a vast number of them. They vary enormously in their status, scope and effectiveness. Broadly speaking, we can divide codes of practice into two categories: statutory codes and self-regulatory codes.

Question: What are statutory codes?

Answer: There are many different types of statutory codes, but what they all have in common is that their creation is invariably sanctioned by an Act of Parliament. Frequently, compliance with the code will be taken into consideration in deciding whether the Act's requirements have been met. The best example is the Highway Code. Although compliance with this Code is not a legal requirement, it will be taken into account in deciding whether an offence has been committed. For example, the Highway Code says that one should look in the mirror before pulling away from the kerb. Failure to do so is not a criminal offence but if, as a result of not looking in the mirror, one has an accident that results in a prosecution for careless driving, then failure to follow the Code will be taken into consideration in deciding whether an offence has taken place.

In sales promotion, the best example of a statutory code is the Code of Practice for Traders on Price Indications, issued under s 25 of the Consumer Protection Act 1987. We look at this further in Chapter 7.

Self-regulation

Question: What are self-regulatory codes?

Answer: These are non-governmental codes, usually issued by a trade association in order to establish and maintain certain standards for members to follow. The Office of Fair Trading (OFT) has always had an obligation to encourage the creation and dissemination of Codes of Practice. The OFT runs a 'Consumer Codes Approval Scheme' under which code sponsors make a promise that their code meets the core criteria of helping consumers identify better businesses and encouraging businesses within the trade to raise their standards of customer service. Recently, the Carpet Foundation became the first trade body within the home furnishings sector to achieve an approved Code of Practice.

Question: Where does the Advertising Standards Authority (ASA) fit into all this?

Answer: The ASA was founded in 1962 as a separate body with an independent chairman and a majority of members independent of the business, to adjudicate on complaints within the British self-regulatory system of advertising control. The system now covers both broadcast and non-broadcast advertising as well as sales promotion and direct marketing. For non-broadcast advertisements, the ASA deals with complaints concerning alleged breaches of the British Code of Advertising, Sales Promotion and Direct Marketing. The ASA is funded by an automatic 0.1% levy on all display advertising, which is collected by the Advertising Standards Board of Finance (ASBOF).The broadcast side of the ASA's work is funded by a separate levy on advertisers of 0.1 per cent of the cost of air time and it is collected by a separate body known as the Broadcast Advertising Standards Board of Finance (BASBOF). A special mailing standards levy is also collected by ASBOF to fund the ASA's work on list and database management.

Question: What, then, is Committee of Advertising Practice (CAP) in relation to non-broadcast advertising?

Answer: 'CAP' is the colloquial way of referring to the Committee of Advertising Practice, which is the industry element in the system of advertising control. Made up of representatives of the various trade associations that support the self-regulatory system, its chief responsibilities are the preparation and review of the Code of Practice, and representing the views of the industry.

Question: What is the Code that CAP is responsible for drafting and keeping under review?

Answer: The British Code of Advertising, Sales Promotion and Direct Marketing, which is a consolidation into a single code of practice designed to regulate marketing communications as a whole the formerly separate rules on advertising, sales promotion and data base management.

Television and radio

Question: Where does television advertising fit into all this?

Answer: Broadcast advertising has, since 2004, been the responsibility of the ASA whereas previously it had been the subject of a separate statutory regime. The Communications Act 2003 gave The Office of Communications (OFCOM) statutory responsibility for broadcasting standards. Using its powers under the Act, OFCOM contracted out responsibility for advertising standards to the ASA in the guise of a separate, but related, body called ASA (Broadcast).

Question: Is there a broadcasting dimension to CAP?

Answer: A separate body known as The Broadcast Committee of Advertising Practice (BCAP) took over responsibility for the pre-existing television and radio advertising codes. Its membership includes representatives from the advertising and marketing industry with an interest in broadcast advertising—advertisers, agencies and television and radio broadcasters.

Question: Where do the Broadcast Advertising Clearance Centre (BACC) and Radio Advertising Clearance Centre (RACC) fit into this?

Answer: The BACC continues its responsibility for pre-clearing television commercials before they are broadcast. Similarly, the RACC continues its pre-clearance function for radio commercials. Both are funded by their broadcaster stakeholders.

CHAPTER 2

THE SELF-REGULATORY CONTROLS EXAMINED

The British Code of Advertising, Sales Promotion and Direct Marketing

Question: Tell me more about the British Code of Advertising, Sales Promotion and Direct Marketing (the Code)

Answer: As to the scope of the Code as it relates to sales promotion, one could not do better than to quote the introductory cll 27.1–27.4

> '27.1 The sales promotion rules must be read in conjunction with the general rules, direct marketing rules and other specific rules, if relevant.
>
> 27.2 The sales promotion rules are designed primarily to protect the public but they also apply to trade promotions and incentive schemes and to the promotional elements of sponsorships. They regulate the nature and administration of promotional marketing techniques. Those techniques generally involve providing a range of direct or indirect additional benefits, usually on a temporary basis, designed to make goods or services more attractive to purchasers. The rules do not apply to the routine, non-promotional, distribution of products or to product extensions, for example the suitability of one-off editorial supplements (be they in printed or electronic form) to newspapers and magazines.
>
> 27.3 Promoters are responsible for all aspects and all stages of promotions.

27.4 Promotions should be conducted equitably, promptly and efficiently and should be seen to deal fairly and honourably with consumers. Promoters should avoid causing unnecessary disappointment.'

Question: How are the sales promotion rules organised?

Answer: After the introduction, the Code's provisions on the protection of consumers, safety and suitability are set out. There then follows general guidelines applying to all forms of sales promotion, as well as rules relating to particular mechanics.

Question: And what about direct marketing rules in the Code?

Answer: As we have noted elsewhere, there is a considerable overlap between sales promotion and direct marketing. However, there are two sets of specific rules in the Code which are of particular relevance to direct marketing. They are the special rules on distance selling in cll 41 and 42, and database practice set out in cl 43, although both topics are now the subject of detailed legal controls which are reflected in the Code provisions.

Note: The Code is set out as Appendix 1.

Question: What are the sanctions of the self-regulatory system?

Answer: The main sanction is publicity, which is achieved through the Advertising Standards Authority (ASA) published adjudications. These receive a wide distribution amongst the press, television, government departments etc. In addition, the Committee of Advertising Practice (CAP) issues media alerts, which advise media proprietors of breaches of the Code, particularly where the advertiser or promoter has not co-operated with the ASA's investigation by not withdrawing or amending a marketing communication that the ASA or CAP has decided breaks the Code. This information is useful to publishers in exercising their discretion as to whether or not to reject advertisement copy—a right which media proprietors have long cherished and which was judicially recognised in the case of *Gamage (A W) Ltd v Temple Press Ltd* [1911].

In addition, the trade associations which support the self-regulatory system make it a requirement of membership that members comply with the Code and with the rulings of the ASA and advice from CAP. CAP member trade bodies also undertake to make sure that marketing campaigns presented for a possible industry award do not infringe the Code.

Question: If I do not like an adjudication from the ASA is there anything that can be done about it?

Answer: There is no formal appeals system as such, but since 1999 there has been a system of 'Independent Review'. The Independent Reviewer at the time of writing is Sir John Caines, a former Permanent Secretary at the Foreign and Commonwealth Office.

A review will be considered only in two situations, which are stipulated in the Code. The first is where there is additional, relevant evidence which was unavailable for submission to the ASA. The second is where a substantial flaw can be shown in the Council's adjudication or in the process by which the adjudication was made.

A review will not be allowed where concurrent legal action is taking place or is contemplated. Where it is allowed, the Reviewer conducts the review with advice from two Assessors—one is the Chairman of the ASA and the other is the Chairman of the Advertising Standards Board of Finance (ASBOF).

The ASA Council will consider the Independent Reviewer's recommendation on a review request that he accepts as meeting the two stipulated criteria but is not obliged to accept it, although it is fair to say that the ASA would have to have good reason not to implement the Reviewer's recommendation.

Question: Can I appeal to one of the CAP panels?

Answer: There are two specialist CAP panels—the General Media Panel and the Sales Promotion and Direct

Response Panel. The Sales Promotion and Direct Response Panel considers a wide range of issues affecting sales promotion and direct marketing and has played a significant role in the creation of a number of CAP notes of guidance, for example on promotions with prizes.

The ASA Executive can and does refer issues to a panel for consideration and it is possible for those who are the subject of an ASA investigation to request that the matter be referred to one of the panels for a review. This is particularly relevant where the complainant raises an issue of general importance or a difficult question in the interpretation of the Codes.

The ASA is not bound to follow the advice of a CAP panel, but since the membership of the panels consists of experts from the industry and from trade associations, their views are persuasive.

Question: What happens if someone feels unaffected by the available sanctions, and decides to ignore the ASA's rulings?

Answer: In cases of misleading advertising—a term which is defined very widely to include sales promotion and direct marketing–the Office of Fair Trading (OFT) has powers under the Control of Misleading Advertisements Regulations 1988, as amended by the Control of Misleading Advertisements (Amendment) Regulations 2000, to secure court orders banning 'misleading advertisements', as well as comparative advertisements that do not meet the requirements set out in the amended regulations. The OFT is empowered to refer complainants to what are termed 'established means', which, for our purposes, will usually be either the trading standards service or the ASA. It is only a tiny number of cases which call for the powers of the OFT, and these usually arise where the ASA either cannot act, or cannot act quickly enough.

It is also worth mentioning that the Enterprise Act 2002 gives the OFT and other enforcement bodies wider powers to obtain court orders against businesses, which do not comply with their legal obligations to consumers. These include a failure to comply with the

Control of Misleading Advertisements Regulations. The OFT can apply for a court order if they are unable, after using their best endeavours, to obtain a satisfactory written assurance from the trader that they will refrain from that course of conduct.

Broadcasters are licensed by the Office of Communications (OFCOM) and the terms of their licence oblige them to broadcast advertisements that comply with the relevant Broadcast Committee of Advertising Practice (BCAP) Code. If a broadcaster does not co-operate, the ASA may refer the matter to OFCOM, which has a range of sanctions at its disposal including fines and the revocation of a licence. These powers are given to OFCOM under the Communications Act 2003.

Question: Can I get advice from CAP?

Answer: Yes. As the industry part of the self-regulatory system CAP offers a comprehensive, free advisory service on all issues relating to the application of the non-broadcast Code.. They can be contacted by telephone on 020 7492 2100, by fax on 020 7404 3404, on the web at www.cap.org.uk and by email on copyadvice@cap.org.uk.

E-commerce

Question: Are there any particular issues with online advertising?

Answer: A particular issue has been advertising virals. These are email, text or other non-broadcast marketing messages that are designed to stimulate significant circulation by recipients and thereby to generate commercial or reputational benefit to the advertiser from the consequential publicity. There is usually a request, either explicit or implicit, for the message to be forwarded to others and sometimes a video clip is attached.

Such marketing activity falls within the operation of the Code. Clause 1.1 makes clear that the Code applies to 'advertisements in ... e-mails, text transmissions ... follow-up literature and other electronic and printed material.'

Accordingly, virals are not excluded from the Code by having originated on a company website or by being forwarded on by consumers. The ASA will judge each complaint on its merits.

Question: Tell me about the WebTrader UK Scheme.

Answer: The Direct Marketing Association (DMA) has created the WebTrader UK Scheme to encourage consumer confidence in the online shopping environment. At the heart of the scheme is a code of practice with which online traders have to comply—a code which reflects legislation and best practice. The scheme is policed, partly by 'Mystery shopping' exercises, monitoring of complaints and customer feedback. The WebTrader UK logo indicates that an online trader is a member of the scheme. Further information can be obtained by e-mailing admin@WebTraderUK.org.uk, or by telephoning 01628 641936.

Question: I have heard about Trust UK. What is it and how does it operate?

Answer: Trust UK acts as an approval body for e-commerce codes, such as those produced by the DMA and by the Association of British Travel Agents (ABTA). Members can display the Trust UK logo on their websites but they must adhere to the terms of their industry codes. The Trust UK e-hallmark ensures that consumers can expect security for payments; protection of data; fair cancellation rights; proper standards of information, delivery and returns; efficient dealing with complaints; and effective redress mechanisms.

Question: What other industry bodies have rules or guidance which are relevant to sales promotion?

Answer: The Institute of Sales Promotion has issued four documents of interest to the sales promotion world. These are 'Notes for guidance on coupons'; 'Guidelines for briefing fulfilment houses'; 'Food product premium inserts'; and 'Prize promotions—guidance notes'. The first two of these documents are set out in Appendices 3 and 4, respectively, below.

The DMA has a Code of Practice, which includes a detailed appendix on sales promotion (discussed in more detail below).

Independent Committee for the Supervision of Standards of Telephone Information Services (ICSTIS)

Question: I have heard about ICSTIS. Does that have a relevance to sales promotion or direct marketing?

Answer: ICSTIS was set up in September 1986, following criticism of the use of some forms of commercial exploitation of premium rate telephone lines—especially in respect of sexually-orientated services. The Committee is an independent watchdog, funded by the telephone companies, to supervise premium or special rate telephone information and entertainment services. It has the power to fine and the power to ban a company from use of the network for a breach of its Code of Practice.

The ICSTIS Code, updated in November 2006, has a section on sales promotion, which should be carefully considered if a promotion is to make use of a special rate 'phone facility'. In particular, the Code requires the rates for a premium rate number to be set out clearly. It is also worth bearing in mind that ICSTIS, like CAP, offers advice on copy clearance.

Other self-regulatory initiatives

Question: Tell me more about the Mailing Preference Service (MPS).

Answer: MPS is an organisation set up in 1983 by the direct mail industry. The service enables members of the public to register their names to be suppressed on all direct marketing lists, or added for all, or any, classes of goods or services. Use of the consumer file by list owners and users is a requirement of the the Code as well as a condition of the DMA Code of Practice.

On a wider basis, the World Convention of MPS facilitates the passing of MPS files between signatories to the Convention, in order to assist companies to avoid mailing to those who do not want to receive direct mail.

Question: What about the Baby MPS?

Answer: The Baby MPS, again set up by the DMA, helps to reduce the number of unwanted baby-related mailings. The scheme is particularly designed to prevent parents being mailed with offers of baby products in the sad circumstances of the death of a baby.

Question: Where does the Telephone Preference Service (TPS) fit in?

Answer: Following the success of the MPS, the DMA was instrumental in setting up the TPS. The TPS was established in 1995 to protect consumers who do not wish to receive unsolicited telephone marketing calls. To make marketing calls when an individual has registered with the TPS that they do not wish to receive such calls from any business or organisation is unlawful under the Privacy and Electronic Communications (European Community Directive) Regulations 2003.

Question: And Fax Preference Service (FPS)?

Answer: Based on the same principle as the MPS and TPS, the FPS enables people operating a fax machine from residential premises to register as not wanting any unsolicited marketing faxes. The service was set up by the DMA, supported by British Telecom (BT) and Mercury Communications.

Question: And what about e-mail?

Answer: Again established by the DMA, the e-MPS enables individuals to register so as not to receive unsolicited marketing information. It is based in the United States and operates globally.

Question: So what is Quality Standard for Mail Production (QMP)?

Answer: The QMP replaced the Direct Mail Accreditation and Recognition Centre (DMARC) in March 2001. QMP is a quality mark awarded to qualifying mailing houses as part of an accreditation scheme developed by the Royal Mail and the DMA.

Question: You mentioned the DMA. What is the role of the DMA in these various self-regulatory initiatives?

Answer: The DMA is responsible for the administration of its Code of Practice and of the MPS, TPS, FPS, QMP and the List Warranty Register under one management division. The DMA adjudicates on any complaints or issues arising from the operation of any of the above functions. The Authority's Chairman sits with the assistance of further independent members, and those members who are appointed from the industry.

Question: So what is this DMA Code?

Answer: Described by a former Director of Consumer Affairs at the Office of Fair Trading as 'a flagship Code and an example to other industries', the Code applies to the direct marketing activities of members of the DMA.

The Code sets out the standards of ethical conduct and best practice that members must adhere to as a condition of DMA membership. Any complaint against a member that cannot be satisfactorily resolved by the complaints officer of the DMA, or where it is requested by either party, is referred to the Direct Marketing Authority.

Question: Can I appeal against a decision of the Direct Marketing Authority?

Answer: Yes, appeals on natural justice grounds are possible from any decision of the Direct Marketing Authority. Appeals lie to an independent Appeals Commissioner.

Question: What is the role of the Royal Mail in relation to self-regulatory initiatives in direct marketing?

Answer: The Royal Mail is particularly significant, since in
                respect of direct mail it is roughly analogous to a
                media owner—but without a media owner's normal
                rights to reject copy. The Royal Mail is a common
                carrier and cannot refuse to carry material unless it
                falls within certain categories set out in section 85 of
                the Postal Services Act 2000. However, the Royal Mail
                can operate a regime which can best be described
                as the withholding of trading privileges. For example,
                under the Mailsort Contract for bulk postage, when a
                discount is given; this discount is tied to compliance
                with appropriate legislation and industry codes.

                Now that the postal delivery market has enabled other
                companies to compete with the Royal Mail, the latter's
                competitors are similarly media owners and, like the
                Royal Mail, are expected to penalise non-compliance
                with relevant codes.

Mail order protection schemes

Question: We want to advertise 'off the page' in national news-
                papers. What must we do?

Answer: You must comply with the National Newspapers'
                Safe Home Ordering Protection Scheme (SHOPS).
                After criticism by the then Consumer Affairs Minis-
                ter, nine Fleet Street publishing houses agreed, in
                1975, to set up a protection scheme for consumers
                responding to mail order advertisements in national
                newspapers under the original name 'Mail Order Pro-
                tection Scheme (MOPS). It is owned jointly by the
                Newspaper Publishers Association and the DMA.

                You will have to join SHOPS. Apart from certain
                exclusions, readers who lose money because of the
                failure of a mail order business are reimbursed from
                a fund to which member advertisers make annual
                contributions. Applications for membership are con-
                sidered by a Managing Committee which requires
                agencies and advertisers to give undertakings and, in
                particular cases, supporting indemnities. You should
                contact the SHOPS secretariat for full particulars of

the scheme and for information about the kinds of obligations and undertakings that would be required.

Question: What are the key requirements for a reader to be protected under SHOPS?

Answer: The consumer will be protected under SHOPS if:

- the advertisement is inserted in a national newspaper;

- the advertiser is in membership of the scheme;

- the advertisement describes a product giving details of price and the address from where it may be obtained;

- the advertisement directly asks for readers to order the product and requests payment in advance.

The over-riding condition that applies is that the advertiser must have been recommended for acceptance into the scheme, and to show this, approved advertisements must include the SHOPS logo in their layout or the SHOPS initials at the bottom of the advertisement.

Question: What about the regional press?

Answer: The Newspaper Society, which represents the regional press, has a scheme designed to make payments where mail order traders have failed to supply goods or refund money and also become the subject of liquidation or bankruptcy proceedings. In certain circumstances, it makes provision for a voluntary payment by the Newspaper Society to the newspaper of up to 50 per cent of any claim refunded to a reader. Use of the scheme is limited to those in membership of the Society.

Within the scope of the Scheme fall direct response display advertisements, both those appearing on run of paper pages and classified pages. Lineage advertisements are excluded.

Question: And what about magazines?

Answer: Magazine publishers who belong to the Periodical Publishers Association (PPA) operate a Protection Scheme to act as a safeguard for their readers. Magazine publishers who do not belong to PPA are not liable for readers' losses. To be included in the PPA scheme, goods must be offered directly off the page in a display or boxed, classified advertisement. Lineage classified advertisements are not covered; nor are loose inserts.

CHAPTER 3

CONTRACTUAL ISSUES AND DISTANCE SELLING

The nature of contracts

Question: What do we mean by a 'contract'?

Answer: For there to be a contract there needs to be three elements present—an offer and acceptance; consideration; and an intention to create legal relations.

Question: What do these terms mean?

Answer: (a) *'Offer and acceptance'*: This means that there must be a clear and definite agreement between both parties, analysed in terms of a definite offer or proposition from one party and a clear unequivocal acceptance from the other.

(b) *'Consideration'*: Every contract must have the presence of consideration. In *Currie v Misa* [1875], it was held that consideration

> 'may consist either in some right, interest, profit, or benefit accruing to the one party, or some forbearance, detriment, loss or responsibility given, suffered, or undertaken by the other'.

An illustration helps: If one party agrees with another to sell them their car for £5,000 there will be consideration and a contract. If one party agrees to give the car away as a gift, there is no consideration and no contract. One important rule is that consideration does not have to be adequate or reasonable—simply that it has value.

(c)   *'Intention to create legal relations'*: This simply means that the parties must intend their agreement to give rise to legal implications. An agreement between a husband and wife will usually not give rise to such an intention, whereas an agreement between business people invariably will.

Question: What is the contractual position when we run a promotion?

Answer: The offer of goods or services with incentives and the acceptance of that offer by a consumer is an enforceable contract and any breach of the terms, conditions or nature of the offer is actionable by the consumer. So too are agreements between sales promotion consultancies and their clients, between promoters and sourcing agencies, and the many other agreements necessary to run a promotion.

Question: What about the terms of the contract?

Answer: There are two main types of contractual term— express and implied. The express terms are those stated expressly in a written contract, in written terms of business and sometimes in correspondence where they are leading up to the contract and the parties intend to be bound by them.

Courts are reluctant to imply terms into a contract, but will do so when it is necessary to give effect to the presumed intention of the parties or to reflect custom and practice in the trade.

Question: Our sales promotion consultancy says in its terms of business that it is a principal at law. What contractual significance does this have?

Answer: In 1931, a survey concluded that practically all advertising agencies regarded themselves as principals and not as agents for either the client or for the media. Since then, a number of decided cases has brought judicial recognition of the custom and practice of the business.

Today, there is little doubt that mainstream marketing communications agencies and public relations agencies contract as principals. So what?

The significance is that, if an agency contracts as principal, it will be bound by the contracts it makes with third parties, be they media, outside creative suppliers, sourcing companies etc. So, for example, if any advertising agency goes into liquidation owing money to a newspaper, that newspaper will have no claim in contract for the debt against the agency's client.

Fulfilment of promotions

Question: We have offered a free set of place mats with our usual range of canteens of cutlery. Due to unexpected demand we have run out of the place mats before the expiry date of the offer. Can we offer different place mats or a price reduction instead?

Answer: This depends on the terms of the offer. If you offered specific place mats up to a definite termination date, then you have a binding contract with any buyer who takes advantage of the offer and you cannot offer other goods or a price reduction in lieu of the place mats. On the other hand, if your promotional literature made it clear that other goods of equivalent value or a price reduction of that value would be given if stocks ran out, you have no problem. These alternatives must be made clear in the original promotion. This is required by the Distance Selling Regulations (see below).

You cannot change the terms of the offer at a later date after you realise that you have insufficient stocks. The British Code of Advertising, Sales Promotion and Direct Marketing (the Code) requires that a genuine attempt should be made to anticipate demand, but in circumstances in which an unexpectedly high level of demand leads to an inability to supply, contingency plans should be made to provide unsuccessful applicants with some alternative item of equivalent or greater value, either in cash or in kind; and the promoter's intention to act thus should be made clear to consumers before they are committed to participation. 'Equivalent value' should be assessed in terms of consumers' likely perceptions of quality and price or cost.

Limitations on offers

Question: What limitations can be placed on an offer of promotional goods other than an expiry date?

Answer: Bearing in mind what we have said above, the normal method of closing an offer is to print 'Offer closes on 21 January' etc prominently on the promotional literature and, where appropriate, on the pack. So far as the law is concerned, the offer could be limited to a specified number of applicants or 'subject to availability'. However, the Code states that promoters are not relieved of the obligation to take all reasonable steps to avoid disappointing the consumer. This rule is modified in respect of genuine 'limited editions' (see below).

Extension of offers

Question: If we have stocks of promotional goods left after the expiry date can we extend the period of the offer?

Answer: Yes, provided all consumers who have applied before the closing date have received their goods and the new extended closing date is clearly stated on all promotional material.

General disclaimers

Question: Can we use words such as 'No refunds can be given if promotional goods are out of stock or are unacceptable'?

Answer: The rights of consumers to reject goods or services that do not conform to a reasonable standard of quality is enshrined in law and cannot be taken away. In addition, it is a criminal offence to exhibit or state a disclaimer that seeks to limit or remove the consumer's rights.

It is not of itself unlawful to try to limit liability where goods cannot be delivered, but such a disclaimer will only be effective insofar as it is 'reasonable'. What is 'unreasonable' must be determined on the facts of each case, but given that the Code frowns on any activity that would lead to consumer disappointment it is likely that a court would rule that such a disclaimer is unreasonable and therefore of no effect.

Delivery

Question: What is the maximum period of delivery of incentive goods after receipt of an application from a consumer?

Answer: There is no specified period in law. Delivery must be within a reasonable period bearing in mind the nature and cost of the goods and the type of promotion involved. However, the Code requires delivery to be within 30 days of application except where the nature of the products concerned makes it impracticable, eg in relation to plants and made to measure products. The Code rule should be adhered to except where it is impracticable, in which case an indication of the different delivery period should be stated in the marketing communication.

Terms of the offer

Question: We wish to make an 'on-pack' offer for free additional goods. What information must appear on the outside of the pack and what can we put on the inside?

Answer: By law the terms of an offer should be clear, unambiguous and easy to understand. If they are not then the contract may be enforced in favour of the consumer. The Code requires that all information that might reasonably affect a consumer's decision to buy must be given before the decision to buy is made. In particular, special attention should be given to any terms or conditions that exclude some consumers from the opportunity to participate in the promotion; impose any geographical limits on eligibility; limit the number of applications permitted; limit the number of promotional products or prizes that an individual or household may claim or win; require additional proofs of purchase; or impose a closing date.

Refunds

Question: Are we under an obligation to refund the purchase price of the principal product when the incentive product is faulty?

Answer: Yes. There is a single contract for the supply of the substantive and promotional products that can be repudiated by the consumer if either should be faulty. The Code requires that promoters should ensure that faulty goods are replaced without delay or that the consumer receives an immediate refund. Where payment has been made by the consumer, the alternative of an exchange of goods cannot be insisted upon.

Misdescription of goods

Question: What are the liabilities of promoters if incentive goods are accidentally misdescribed?

Answer: If the goods do not conform to any description of them, the consumer has the right to reject them and get his or her money back. If the description is false to a material degree, an offence against the Trade Descriptions Act 1968 (the 1968 Act) may have been committed. This Act creates offences of strict liability and it is no defence that the misdescription is accidental.

Question: Are there any rules about the presentation of promotional information?

Answer: It is implicit in the Code that all necessary promotional information is presented in a manner that is easy to understand and not misleading. So far as the law is concerned, information that, although complete in itself, is confusing, would be likely to render a contract unenforceable. More important perhaps is the judgment in *Read Bros Cycles (Leyton) Ltd v Waltham Forest London Borough Council* [1978] where all the information necessary for consumers to understand the offer was given but was split between advertisements and notices and was generally confusing. The court held that an offence concerning a misleading indication of price (see Chapter 7 below) was committed.

Unfair contracts

Question: What about legislation on unfair contracts?

Answer: The Unfair Contract Terms Act 1977 imposes major controls on the use of exclusion clauses in contracts. Exclusion clauses are those terms designed to restrict or remove the liability that would otherwise ensue for breach of contract.

In addition, the Unfair Terms in Consumer Contracts Regulations 1999 provide that an unfair term in a consumer contract is not binding on the consumer. An unfair term is one which, contrary to the requirement of good faith, causes a significant imbalance in the parties' rights and obligations under the contract to the detriment of the consumer. Schedule 2 to the Regulations contain a non-exhaustive list of matters which may be regarded as unfair.

The Regulations also provide that the Office of Fair Trading (OFT) shall consider any complaint made about the fairness of any contract term drawn up for general use. The OFT may, if they consider it appropriate to do so, seek an injunction to prevent the continued use of that term or a term having like effect in contracts drawn up for general use by a party to the proceedings.

Criminal law and failure to fulfil offers

Question: Is it an offence under the 1968 Act if the offer of incentive goods or services is not fulfilled?

Answer: Generally speaking there is no offence in criminal law where incentive goods are offered but not supplied. The enforcement authorities have unsuccessfully attempted to employ s 14(1)(b) of the 1968 Act to prosecute cases where this has happened. That offence concerns the reckless making of a statement which is false as to the provision of a service. In *Kinchin v Ashton Park Scooters Ltd* [1984], for example, it was held that the failure to provide free gifts offered on the purchase of a motor scooter was outside the scope of the Act. Again, in *Dixons Ltd v Roberts* [1984] it was held that failure to provide a refund claimed in consequence of an advertised offer to 'refund the difference if you buy Dixon's Deal products cheaper locally at any time of purchase and call within seven days' was not an offence under the Act. Similarly, in *Newell and Taylor v Hicks* [1983] it was held that failure to provide free video recorders with every purchase of a car was not an offence. However, in *Warwickshire County Council v Dixons* [1993], it was held that a failure to honour a price promise can give rise to liability for a misleading price indication under Pt III of the Consumer Protection Act 1987.

It should be borne in mind that all of these cases would have been actionable at civil law, even where there is no criminal liability, and all, of course, are breaches of the Code.

Quality of promotional goods

Question: Are there any requirements as to the quality of promotional goods?

Answer: In all sales of goods there is an implied term about quality by virtue of the Sale and Supply of Goods Act 1994 (the 1994 Act). Under s 1 of that Act, where the seller sells goods in the course of business, there is an implied term that the goods are of satisfactory quality. 'Satisfactory quality' is defined as goods meeting the standard that a reasonable person would regard as satisfactory—taking into account the description, the price and all other relevant circumstances.

The 1994 Act says that the quality of goods includes their state and condition of the goods, and gives examples of factors which, in appropriate cases, can be regarded as aspects of the quality of goods:

(a)   fitness for all the purposes for which goods of the kind in question are commonly supplied;

(b)   appearance and finish;

(c)   freedom from minor defects;

(d)   safety; and

(e)   durability.

If these conditions of contract are not fulfilled, the buyer may reject the goods within a reasonable period after purchase and ask for his or her money back. Any offer of an exchange of goods or credit notes may be accepted at the discretion of the buyer but cannot be insisted upon.

It should always be remembered that non-conformity with description may also be a criminal offence under the 1968 Act.

The Code requires that all promotional products meet satisfactory standards of safety, durability and performance in use. When applicable, such matters as guarantees and the availability of servicing should be clearly explained.

The quality of services

Question: Where offers such as 'free fitting' or '12 months free service' are made, are there any requirements as to the quality of such services?

Answer: As in the case of goods above, the law imposes certain implied conditions in all consumer contracts. These conditions are:

- The supplier will carry out the service with reasonable care and skill. The degree of care and skill is that which a reasonably competent person in the particular trade or industry could be expected to have. In such cases, the promoter is liable for any defective work carried out by his or her own or contracted employees.

- The service must be carried out within a reasonable time. Unless the contract specifies a time when the work will be carried out there is an implied term that the work will be completed within a reasonable time. What is reasonable is a question of fact in every case but in the typical 'free fitting' promotion the period will be a matter of hours or days so that the buyer can make almost immediate use of the product.

Suitability of promotional products

Question: Are there any precautions of which promoters should be aware as to sensitive product groups for consumers?

Answer: It need hardly be said that obscenity should be avoided, but it is often not understood that it is unlawful to send to any person any book, magazine or leaflet which is unsolicited and which describes or illustrates human sexual techniques.

In more general terms, the Code states that promoters should not offer promotional products that are of a nature likely to cause offence or products that, in the context of the promotion, may reasonably be considered to be socially undesirable. Promoters are required to take special care with promotional products, the distribution of which is subject to any form of legal restriction. Particular care should also be taken in the distribution of free samples to ensure that children or other particularly vulnerable groups are not harmed.

Question: Are there any particular issues in respect of consumer guarantees as to quality?

Answer: Yes, the Consumer Transactions (Restrictions on Statements) Order 1976, as amended by the Consumer Transactions (Restrictions on Statements) (Amendment) Order 1978, makes it a criminal offence to make any statement about the obligations accepted by the supplier in respect of goods being defective, not fit for purpose or, not corresponding with description, unless a statement is made to the effect that the consumer's statutory rights are not affected. In practice, it is sufficient to simply say 'Statutory rights not affected' in close proximity to any statement about quality, particularly in relation to a consumer guarantee.

Unsolicited goods and services

Question: What are the constraints on sending out unsolicited incentives?

Answer: Goods are unsolicited if they are sent out without any prior request from the recipient. There is nothing to prevent the despatch of unsolicited incentives which are not specifically forbidden by law on grounds of taste or safety (eg explosive or flammable goods, material on sexual techniques etc). However, under the Unsolicited Goods and Services Act 1971 (the 1971 Act), as amended by the Consumer Protection (Distance Selling) Regulations 2000, and the Unsolicited Goods and Services Act 1971 (Electronic Commerce) (Amendment) Regulations 2005, no payment of any kind may be demanded and there is no right to such payment, provided the recipient retains them for collection for a period of six months or gives 30 days' notice of such availability before the end of the six-month period. Thereafter, the goods become an unconditional gift to the recipient.

Limited editions

Question: It greatly enhances the desirability of a product if it is called a 'limited edition'. What controls are there on the use of this technique?

Answer: The Code allows editions to be limited by the number produced provided the promotion material clearly states the maximum number to be produced and the terms of the offer are in all respects clearly stated. The Code gives only grudging approval to editions limited by time, ie by the number of persons applying within a stated period of time. In such cases the word 'limited' or any of its derivatives may not be used without qualification and the advertiser must advertise its willingness to inform all interested purchasers of the number of articles eventually produced worldwide.

A statement in promotional literature that applications should be received by a certain date is not of itself the offer of a limited edition, but difficulties have been experienced in the interpretation of the Code in this respect.

Identity of the promoter

Question: What are the rules about revealing the identity of promoters in promotional literature? Could we, for example, show only the name of our handling agents, omitting any reference to ourselves?

Answer: Concealment of the true identity of a promoter would be contrary to the Code, which requires that full information shall be given in relation to all promotions and that promotions shall be fair and honest. The Advertising Standards Authority has adjudicated against a number of promotions where the promoter's proper name and address have not been given.

So far as the law is concerned, the contracting party would be that party named in the promotional material. It therefore follows that any action brought by a consumer would be against the company whose name appeared in the promotional material.

Question: But what about the situation where we use a travel company—cannot we give their name?

Answer: There is nothing wrong in giving the name of, for example, a travel company for the purpose of dealing with detailed questions concerning flights and hotels and questions of that sort. But under the Code the promoter remains responsible for all aspects of the promotion and, whilst a company can delegate some aspects of the execution of the promotion, it cannot delegate its overall responsibility.

Distance selling regulations

Question: There are detailed regulations affecting distance selling. What is distance selling?

Answer: The Consumer Protection (Distance Selling) Regulations 2000 (as amended) apply to 'distance contracts' which are defined as:

> 'any contract concerning goods or services concluded between a supplier and a consumer under an organised distance sales or service provision scheme run by the supplier who, for the purpose of the contract makes exclusive use of one or more means of distance communication up to and including the moment at which the contract is concluded'.

'Means of distance communication' is defined as 'any means which, without the simultaneous physical presence of the supplier and the consumer, may be used for the conclusion of a contract between those parties'.

So, clearly, mail order trading is covered and so too would be self-liquidator and similar offers in the world of sales promotion.

Question: Are there any exemptions from the new Regulations?

Answer: There are a number of exemptions, including vending machines, contracts with telecommunications operators by public payphone, immoveable property rights and auctions. There are also some partial exemptions: in particular, information and the right of cancellation does not apply to regular deliveries to home and work for everyday consumption, such as milk and newspapers. Also excluded are contracts for leisure, transport or accommodation or catering on specific dates. There are also specific exceptions to the right of cancellation, as we shall see later.

Question: What information has to be given and when?

Answer: Before or at the time of concluding the contract the consumer must be informed of the identify of the supplier, the main characteristics of the goods, the price, arrangements for delivery and the closing date, as well as the fact that the consumer has the right of cancellation under reg 13 of the Regulations, where applicable. Also, if the supplier intends to substitute goods of equivalent quality and price in the event of supply problems, this needs to be made clear.

Question: What is the 'right to cancel'?

Answer: Under the Regulations, consumers have the right to cancel a distance contract any time from the date of the conclusion of the contract—and for up to seven clear working days after delivery. Consumers must then be reimbursed within 30 days.

Question: Are there any exceptions from the right to cancel?

Answer: Yes:

  (a)   supplies of services that have, with the consent of the customer, commenced within a seven-working-day period;

  (b)   where the price is dependent on fluctuations in the financial market which the supplier cannot control;

(c)   goods made to the customer's specifications, or clearly personalised, or subject to a short shelf-life;

(d)   audio and video recordings or computer software, if they are unsealed by the consumer;

(e)   newspapers, periodicals and magazines;

(f)   gaming, betting and lottery services.

Question: How do I express the right to withdraw?

Answer: There has been much discussion on this, but I believe the following wording is the best and most succinct way of expressing the right to cancel: 'You can cancel under this contract up to seven clear working days from delivery by returning, at your own cost, the item to the promoter'.

Question: How do I express the right to substitute other goods?

Answer: I suggest something along the following lines: 'The promoter may substitute an equivalent item if the one requested is unavailable. If you wish to cancel and return the substituted item, your costs will be refunded'.

Question: What happens if I do not comply with the requirements as to information provided by the Regulations?

Answer: The cooling-off period can be extended by three months from the date it would have expired had notice been given.

Contracts away from business premises

Question: What other statutory restrictions exist on direct selling?

Answer: In relation to consumer credit, canvassing business door-to-door requires a licence, and it is a criminal offence to canvass for what are called 'debtor–creditor agreements'—a term which covers most forms of cash loan.

Provisions under consumer credit legislation also provide for certain 'cooling-off' and cancellation rights in respect of credit agreements negotiated away from business premises.

There is legislation giving a more general right to cancel in distance selling agreements in the form of the Consumer Protection (Cancellation of Contracts Concluded away from Business Premises) Regulations 1987.

Question: Tell me more about the Consumer Protection (Cancellation of Contracts Concluded away from Business Premises) Regulations 1987.

Answer: The rights under these Regulations apply when the consumer agrees to buy goods or services from a trader as a result of an unsolicited visit to the consumer's home or place of work. They also apply where a consumer, having asked the trader to call, agrees to buy other goods, the identity of which were not, at that stage, known to the consumer.

Traders are required to give their customers written notice that they have a seven-day cooling-off period during which agreements covered by the Regulations can be cancelled without penalty. The notice from the trader must also specify the name and address of the company or person against whom the right of cancellation can be exercised.

Question: Are there any relevant Codes covering this area?

Answer: Yes. The Direct Selling Association (DSA) is the author of a consumer code of practice. The DSA was established in 1965 and its member companies account for 59per cent of those involved in the direct selling channel of distribution. The Code provides consumers with a level of protection that exceeds their legal rights and it has been approved by the OFT. There is an independent Code Administrator whose judgments are binding on all members.

E-commerce

Question:	Many contracts are now concluded electronically. What do the Regulations say?
Answer:	The Electronic Commerce (EC Directive) Regulations 2002 provides that those engaged in e-commerce must provide the following general information:

(a) the business name, geographic address and other relevant details including e-mail address;

(b) details of any publicly available register in which you are entered, together with your registration number or equivalent;

(c) the particulars of any supervisory body if there is any relevant scheme of authorisation in place;

(d) details of any professional body with which the trader is registered;

(e) the Trader's VAT registration number.

For those contracting online, customers must be given information about:

(a) the technical steps required to conclude the contract;

(b) whether the finalised contract will be filed by the trader and whether in this form it will be accessible;

(c) the relevant language or languages offered for the conclusion of the contract;

(d) any relevant codes of conduct to which the trader subscribes together with information as to how these may be accessed.

Question:	What about trading disclosures?

Answer: The Companies (Registrar, Languages and Trading
                   Disclosures) Regulations 2006 require that all com-
                   panies in the United Kingdom must clearly state the
                   company registration number, place of registration
                   and registered office address on all company web-
                   sites. If the company is being wound up, that fact
                   needs to be made clear on the website as well.

CHAPTER 4

PRIZE PROMOTIONS

Background

Question: The law in this area has recently changed—why?

Answer: A sea change has taken place in the attitude of our society to lotteries and other games of chance. Historically, lotteries in particular, were seen as a way of exploiting the poor. In the case of *Reader's Digest v Williams* 1976, the then Lord Chief Justice observed that the purpose of the law had been to prevent those poor people who only had a few pence to buy food for their children from losing money. The law until 2007 reflected this view.

Question: Why the change?

Answer: The change has been a reflection of changed attitudes. Many factors are responsible. The launch of the National Lottery was one of the most significant because gambling ceased to be a minority pursuit and instead became an activity in which the majority of the population had participated to some degree. An activity once seen as a risk to the poor and disadvantaged had suddenly become a significant part of the leisure industry.

Question: But what about promotional marketing?

Answer: The situation was unsatisfactory. Linking games of chance directly to product purchase, as with an instant win, gave rise to the spectre of an illegal lottery. To cope with the legal problem, free entry routes were developed so that nobody was obliged to purchase. But this was never sanctioned by either statute or by case law. Legally doubtful, its acceptance was simply a part of a policy laid down by the Crown Prosecution Service (CPS). The public never understood why chances were given to non-purchasers. It was clear that the public did not understand why promotional games of chance linked to the purchase of goods or services were tainted with illegality and this was much of the reasoning behind the CPS policy not to challenge such promotions if there was a genuine and realistic free entry route.

As a result of a comprehensive review of gambling legislation, the Government made the Gambling Act 2005.

Promotional games of chance

Question: I am told that the Act has introduced the New Zealand model. What does this mean?

Answer: New Zealand was used as a model for reform in the United Kingdom. In New Zealand, games of chance were allowed in relation to product purchase without the need for a free entry route. The Gambling Act introduces the same approach into UK law. It does this by re-defining 'lottery' so as not to include a produce purchase obligation. For the first time, there is a statutory definition of lottery, but one based on previous case law—essentially the offer of prizes in a game of chance in which people are required to pay in money or money's worth in order to participate. However, Sch 2(2) makes it clear that an obligation to pay for goods or services will not count as payment within the definition of a lottery unless one is paying at a price or rate which reflects the opportunity to participate. In other words, it is only if the price is 'loaded' to take account of the promotion that the scheme will contribute an illegal lottery.

Question: What is the effect of this on promotional marketing?

Answer: It means that unless the price has been inflated on account of the promotion, any promotional game of chance is legal without the need for a free entry route.

Question: What about postage or telephone costs?

Answer: The Act makes it clear that the ordinary cost of postage or telephone calls will not constitute payment. However, if the cost is more than the basic, as in the case of a premium rate 'phone call, it will be regarded as payment. This reflects the understanding which grew up in relation to the previous legislation.

Question: What happens if a charge is made, not for formal entry into a prize promotion, but in order to ascertain whether one has won and, if so, the identity of the prize?

Answer: Both situations are covered in paras 6 and 7 of Sch 2 of the Act. Any payment in order to discover whether a prize has been won or to claim a prize will be regarded as a payment to take part in the arrangement making such schemes lotteries.

Question: But what if I offered a 50 per cent discount off the price of a world cruise? Does that mean my promotion will be an illegal lottery?

Answer: This was a question which troubled many of us before the Bill was passed. And it is an issue that encompasses many other situations. What is the position, for example, in relation to a prize of a ticket to a pop concert where one has to pay the cost of travel to the event. And what about a car that will need to be taxed and issued before it can be driven?

When Ministers were challenged on this they argued that such arrangements did not contravene the statutory provisions. They argued that where a 50 per cent voucher was the prize, one took possession of the prize when one received the voucher. They argued similarly in relation to the other examples. More importantly, perhaps, this view appears to have been taken also by the Gambling Commission—the dedicated enforcement body under the Act. Since they are responsible for enforcement, one can presumably take a relaxed view of the issue.

Question: What is the difference between a prize and a gift?

Answer: I do not know of any case law defining the term 'prize' in contradistinction to 'gift'. The British Code of Advertising, Sales Promotion and Direct Marketing does not define 'prize', but says that gifts offered to all or most participants should not be described as prizes. Accordingly, if everyone 'wins' something of comparable value, it is a gift and not a prize.

Question: What if a retailer offers, say, to refund the purchase price to all those who spend £50 or more in their shop during the month of May if England subsequently wins the World Cup that year?

Answer: It has always seemed to me that such a scheme is not caught by the legislation on lotteries, because either everyone will receive something, or everyone will receive nothing. Each purchaser stands in exactly the same position as all other purchasers. There is no drawing of lots which would suggest that prizes are to be distributed to each winner according to chance. The outcome of the World Cup is determined by the skill of the teams and is not, therefore, a result based on chance.

This scheme clearly is not a competition, because of the absence of any skill or dexterity by participants. Neither can the participants said to be playing a game. This rules out the application of gaming legislation.

However, the conundrum lies in whether such a promotion can be said to be a wager or a bet. When the Institute of Sales Promotion sought leading counsel's advice on this point, his advice was that such a promotion did not fit into case law definitions of 'wager' and 'bet'.

The final arbiter of such matters will be the courts. However, given the backing of leading counsel's opinion, I see no reason why promoters should be dissuaded from running such promotions.

Question: What is the situation if participants did not appreciate that they acquired a chance when they spent money?

Answer: It used to be the case that if people spent money unaware that they were obtaining a chance, that payment did not constitute contribution from the point of view of the definition of a lottery. This principle arose in the case of *Minty v Sylvester* in 1915, the basis of which was if that there was no 'allurement' there was no contribution. The ruling in *Minty v Sylvester* has now been done away with as a result of Sch 2, para 4, which says 'It is also immaterial for the purposes of s 14 and this Schedule whether a person knows when he makes a payment that he thereby participates in an arrangement.'

Question: I have heard about customer lotteries. What are they?

Answer: The Government has established a new category of exempt lottery. Apart from traditional exemptions for the National Lottery, private lotteries and society lotteries, there is a new category of 'customer lottery'. This is a lottery promoted by a person who occupies business premises provided that nobody wins more than £50 as a prize and the lottery is organised in such a way as to ensure that no profits are made. It is therefore a small non-profit making method of creating interest for customers.

Games of chance and National Lottery tickets

Question: What about games of chance and other promotions which make reference to the National Lottery?

Answer: Many promotions have referred to the National Lottery, in ways too varied to describe in detail. They range from 'Sorry you were not successful, but your ticket is worth 50p off your grocery bill this week' to 'You may not have won on the Lottery with only one number, but with us you have won ... ', etc. The law is in s 16 of the National Lottery etc. Act 1993, which prohibits any false indication that a scheme is part of the National Lottery or otherwise connected with it.

The problem is what is meant by 'otherwise connected with it'. Personally, I think it means any false suggestion of an official link; for example, a suggestion that Camelot has licensed the scheme in some way. It is a difficult area and each scheme has to be looked at separately.

What one can say is that if a promoter is in doubt, it is probably a good idea to institute a formal disclaimer such as 'This promotion is not connected with the National Lottery in any way whatsoever'. Such disclaimers have been used in respect of some promotions in the tabloid press.

Question: What about National Lottery tickets as prizes and as premiums?

Answer: The thorniest issue, and the one with the greatest impact on the promotions industry, is the question of giving National Lottery tickets or scratchcards as prizes or premiums. Dealing in Lottery tickets is prohibited under the terms of Camelot's licence to run the National Lottery and under the published game rules, and the view has been taken that buying Lottery tickets and giving them away in a promotion would amount to dealing in Lottery tickets.

At a meeting, Camelot told me that they may not pay out in respect of prizes won on promotional Lottery tickets or scratchcards. The courts have not ruled on this issue but I, for one, would not be prepared to take the risk.

Games of skill

Question: What does the Act say about competitions?

Answer: Very little in fact. The Act is solely concerned with gambling in its various forms. Accordingly s 339 provides that a prize competition is not gambling for the purposes of the Act unless it is either:

(a)   gaming within the mean of s 6;

(b) participation in a lottery within the meaning of s 14; or

(c) betting within the meaning of ss 9–11.

Question: When will a prize promotion amount to gaming?

Answer: Section 6 tells us that gaming means playing a game of chance for a prize. Playing a game was taken by the Gaming Board, and presumably will also be taken by the Gambling Commission, to mean a proactive game rather than one involving merely passive participation. The former would cover, for example, a game involving throwing a dice or spinning a wheel, whereas the latter might involve merely rubbing off a scratchcard.

Question: When will a prize promotion amount to a lottery?

Answer: This is more complicated. Section 14(5) provides:

'A process which requires persons to exercise skill or judgment or to display knowledge shall be treated for the purposes of this section as relying wholly on chance if

(a) the requirement cannot reasonably be expected to prevent a significant proportion of persons who participate in the arrangement of which the process forms part from receiving a prize, and

(b) the requirement cannot reasonably be expected to prevent a significant proportion of persons who wish to participate in that arrangement from doing so.'

Question: What does this amount to?

Answer: It means that what is supposedly a game of skill will be regarded as a game of chance if the skill required cannot reasonably be expected to prevent a significant proportion of participants from winning a prize or from wishing to participate. How this will be interpreted in practice remains to be seen. Much will depend on the practical enforcement approach of the Gambling Commission and any case law.

Question: What about multi-stage promotions?

Answer: This was always the most difficult aspect of the old law and in many ways remains so. If the first stage relies wholly on chance, the whole scheme will be regarded as a game of chance. If it is another stage, then the test enunciated in the previous question has to be applied. If that test is not satisfied, then again the whole prize promotion will be regarded as a game of chance.

Question: When will a prize promotion amount to betting?

Answer: Under the old law, the forecasting of the result of a future event or of a past event, the result of which was not yet ascertained or generally known, would make a prize promotion an illegal competition. In the new law, that element is reflected within the statutory provisions on betting. Betting, in s 9, is defined as:

> ' ... making or accepting a bet on
>
> (a) the outcome of a race, competition or other event or process;
>
> (b) the likelihood of anything occurring or not occurring; or
>
> (c) whether anything is or is not true.'

Particular types of competition

Question: What about 'spot the ball' competitions?

Answer: The legal status of 'spot the ball' competitions was never satisfactorily and definitively settled under the old law. The problem is that whilst skill would probably get you to the general area in which the ball is located, where precisely the ball is must be a matter of pure chance.

In view of the wide preponderance of 'spot the ball' type schemes and the absence of any clear challenge on the point of legality it is probably safe, in practice, to run such schemes. However, the best advice may be to ask competitors where the ball most logically would be, rather than where the ball actually was. However, the author believes that spot the ball competitions, however they are run, are likely to satisfy the test of skill set out in s 14(5) of the Gambling Act 2005.

Question: Do ranking competitions present any special problems?

Answer: Ranking competitions, or factoral competitions as they are sometimes known, involve putting a list of factors in order of importance. They are a popular form of competition, but they pose problems for both consumers and promoters alike.

Depending on the number of factors, it can be virtually impossible to win a ranking competition due to the huge number of possible variants. Some unscrupulous competition organisers have, therefore, organised ranking competitions knowing the chances of winning are infinitesimally small. They then offer a substantial prize, say £1 million, and cover the very slight risk of winning by means of an insurance policy.

To deal with this problem, the Committee of Advertising Practice has advised that, if some advertised prizes may not be won, this fact should be made clear, and if the winning of a prize is distinctly unlikely that fact should be given special prominence.

It is advisable for a promoter to give a small pen picture of the sort of person whose judgment would be relevant to the list of factors. So, instead of saying 'List these factors in order of importance', one should be more specific, eg 'List these factors in order of importance from the point of view of the modern busy housewife'. This makes the competition more focused. It is then less open to the danger of the scheme being regarded as illegal, as happened in the case of *Hobbs v Ward* in 1929 where the court concluded that all one could do to take part was to make a guess at the right order.

Finally, in ranking competitions promoters should ensure, if they are awarding prizes to nearly correct listings, that this is to be judged in descending order. There is a lot of difference between the transposing of the bottom two factors and the transposing of the top two.

Question: And what about estimating-type competitions?

Answer: Competitions that involve estimating distances and amounts are particularly problematic in that their judging is much more likely to be challenged. One professional 'comper' regularly challenges the judging of estimating-type questions, particularly when they involve distances between two points. There is no reason in law why a promoter should not run such a competition, but it should be aware of the risks. It is very important to avoid describing the outcome of the judges' deliberation as 'the right answer' or 'the correct answer': there will be people who will have bought thousands of bars of chocolate just to see how many fit into the back of a Mini. Accordingly, promoters should make it clear that it is the answer as determined by the panel of judges, and that the judges' decision is final.

The position now of free entry routes

Question: How important are the changes?

Answer: It would be no exaggeration to say it is the most profound change to the regulatory framework affecting promotional marketing ever. Certainly by effectively allowing lotteries in sales promotion it will have major consequences for the business. Most importantly it means the end of the necessity for free entry routes in relation to on-pack games of chance such as instant wins. This change is further likely to diminish the use of skill competitions in the industry, particularly since, as a rule, games of chance can be easier to administer and bring a greater response.

In fact, the legislation creates for promotional marketing a very unrestricted environment. As we have seen, the consequence of not meeting the skill test in the Act is that a promotion is seen totally as chance and not skill. Similarly, where the first stage is chance the whole promotion is seen as chance. However, as we have also seen, provided the price of a product or service is not 'loaded' such promotions are legal in any event. What this means is that provided the price of a product is not increased on account of the promotion, then any combination of skill or chance will be legal.

Question: What about premium rate promotions?

Answer: In any case where under the terms of the Act there will still be payment to take part, a game of chance will constitute a lottery. The best example of this is the case of a premium rate promotion. Not being the basic cost of a telephone call, the additional will be regarded as payment and in the context of a game of chance such as a draw this will make the scheme a lottery. The only way to avoid a lottery arising is to institute a free entry route.

Question: I thought free entry routes were no longer needed?

Answer: For most purposes, yes. But in a few cases it will be the only way to prevent a scheme constituting an illegal lottery. Paragraph 8 of Sch 2 provides that an arrangement is not to be regarded as a lottery if there is a genuine choice to pay or not pay. The promoter's alternative route must not involve charging more than the ordinary cost of a letter. Alternatively, it can involve another method of communication which is neither more expensive nor less convenient than paying to enter the promotion. Some might reasonably argue that a free entry route is always less convenient than buying a product. A practical view is called for from the Gambling Commission and the courts.

Contractual issues

Question: The Gambling Act 2005 gives rise to a criminal prosecution. Are there no civil law implications in respect of competitions?

Answer: Yes. When people enter a competition there is a contract between the participant and the promoter. This is one reason why it is so important to spend time on drafting the rules of the competition. Even free-entry competitions can create a contractual relationship if some 'consideration' is involved. Breach of contract could be occasioned by a failure to run the competition properly, for example, by failing to follow the published methodology for selecting winners. For instance, in the case of *Chaplin v Hicks* [1911] a woman was awarded damages for the loss of a chance to win a beauty contest; she had lost that chance because of a breach of contract by the organisers.

Since the rules set out the basis of the contract between the promoter and the consumer it is important to ensure total accuracy. Promoters have come unstuck by claiming that a panel of judges was independent when only one member was. And do not say 'Proof of postage will not be taken as proof of delivery' if what you mean is 'Proof of posting will not be taken as proof of delivery'.

Another area of civil law that may be relevant is product liability. If a product supplied as a prize is defective and causes injury then a civil action will lie.

Competition rules

Question: Now I have established the basic legality of my promotion. What's next?

Answer: You must next make sure that the scheme meets all the requirements of the British Code of

Advertising, Sales Promotion and Direct Marketing ('the Code').

Question: What about the rules of the promotion?

Answer: Clauses 34 and 35 of the Code give guidance on the construction of rules for competitions and other promotions with prizes. Getting the rules right is critically important for the interests of the promoter, as well as the consumer. Many subsequent arguments could have been avoided if more attention had been given to getting the rules set out clearly, comprehensively and unambiguously. The issues that should be covered by the rules are as follows:

(a) the closing date;

(b) any restriction on the number of entries or prizes that may be won;

(c) any requirements for proof of purchase;

(d) description of prizes;

(e) any age or other personal restrictions, or any geographical restrictions;

(f) how and when winners will be notified and results published;

(g) the criteria for judging entries;

(h) where appropriate, the ownership of copyright in entries;

(i) whether and how entries are returnable by the promoter;

(j) how participants may obtain any supplementary rules which may apply—although these should not be rules which would reasonably affect the decision to purchase in the first place;

(k) if a cash alternative to any prize is available;

(l)   any permissions required, eg from parent or employer;

(m)   any intention to use winners in related publicity.

Finally, in common with all promotions there should be a clear statement of the promoter's name and normal business address.

Question: Can I short-circuit the process?

Answer: Sometimes it may not be possible to include all the necessary rules, and competitors may have to be directed towards an address from which they can get the full rules. If this is done, the rules given 'up-front' must be those which have a direct bearing on whether the consumer decides to purchase and participate in the promotion. The Code says that the items which should be made clear before purchase or participation are:

(a)   the closing date for receipt of entries;

(b)   any geographical or personal restrictions such as location or age;

(c)   any requirements for proofs of purchase;

(d)   the need, if applicable, to obtain permission to enter from parents, employers or others;

(e)   the nature of the prize(s);

(f)   the identity of the promoter.

Changing the goal posts

Question: What happens if I realise that I have misjudged things after the promotion has started?

Answer: Usually there is little that can be done. Sometimes the competition does not generate enough interest, for any number of reasons. Even so, the competition must be completed and prizes awarded—even if all the entrants qualify for prizes. Slippage of dates may be excusable if there is some good reason for it. Although it will rarely, if ever, be acceptable to delay the closing date, the date by which winners will be notified may slip because of unforeseeable circumstances. However, unless there is a very good reason indeed, such slippages could result in an infringement of the Code.

In addition, it is worth remembering, as we have already noted, that when competitors take part in a promotional competition there is a legally binding contract between the participants and the promoter. The rules are part of the contract and failure to abide by them is a breach of contract.

A single prize

Question: Should a promoter continue to advertise a prize promotion, such as an instant win, knowing that the only prize has already been claimed and is therefore no longer available to be won.

Answer: This is a difficult question in practice. It is the reason why some promoters have been known to make sure that the winning scratchcard only makes its appearance towards the end of the promotion. What one can say is that there should be several other valuable prizes within the promotion so that if a main prize is claimed there is still a legitimate reason to continue with the promotion.

Publicity

Question: How can I try to ensure that I get a publicity return from my promotion?

Answer: Two rules are particularly relevant here:

(1) It is important to state, as required by the Code, whether or not there is a cash alternative to the prize. Failure to make it clear that there is no cash alternative to a prize has in the past led some competitors to refuse to attend a ceremony for the award of a prize.

(2) The rules should, if appropriate, state that winners may be, or will be, required to take part in related publicity.

CHAPTER 5

DATA PROTECTION ISSUES

Introduction

Question: What, in a nutshell, is the objective of data protection legislation?

Answer: Concern about the use of computers for the collecting, storing, processing and distribution of personal information lay behind the establishment of a European Convention on Data Protection. The purpose of UK data protection legislation was therefore to enable the UK government to meet its obligations under the European Convention, as well as addressing growing concerns about computers and personal information.

Question: What does the Data Protection Act 1998 (the 1998 Act) cover?

Answer: Broadly speaking, the 1998 Act covers information relating to identifiable living people, whether held in a computer or a manual filing system so long as it is relatively easy to extract information about the individuals. The 1998 Act applies both to data controlled by individuals as well as by organisations. Those who control the processing of personal data are, not surprisingly, known as 'data controllers'. And those who process data on behalf of a data controller are termed 'data processors'.

Question: What is meant by notification?

Answer: The 1998 Act provides for a system of 'notification'. If you control the processing of personal data you must notify the Information Commissioner, which involves setting out where you obtained the data from and the uses to which you intend to put it.

Question: How does this affect particular elements in the list business?

Answer: There are several players in the creation and use of mailing lists. First, there is the list owner, who creates the list and makes it available. Secondly, there are the third parties to whom the list is made available, such as a list broker. Thirdly, there may be a direct marketing agency involved. Fourthly—last but not least—is the advertiser whose mailing shot is to be sent to those on the list.

As far as the 1998 Act is concerned, it applies first to the list owner, since it will normally have created the list and, having computerised it, will be its controller. List brokers may need to notify under the Act depending on whether they control the contents of the list. If brokers only arrange the use of lists and have no control over them, they do not need to notify, and the same is true of the direct marketing agency. It is also true of the advertiser unless the advertiser comes to control the list—and an advertiser can quite easily come to control a list if it keeps a bought-in list on computer and operates a suppression mechanism. They would then have the same responsibilities as a list owner.

Finally, mailing houses, because they are processing automatically personal data for third parties, may need to notify.

Question: Who is the Information Commissioner?

Answer: The Information Commissioner is appointed by the Queen on the recommendation of the government of the day. The Information Commissioner must give an annual report to Parliament. The Information Commissioner's functions under the 1998 Act are, principally, to compile and maintain the Register of Data Controllers and to promote compliance with the Data Protection Principles. In addition, the Information Commissioner has the role of encouraging codes of practice in particular sectors, and of assisting in compliance with the Data Protection Principles. Finally, there is certain enforcement action that the Information Commissioner can take, which may involve enforcement notices in relation to the Data Protection Principles, or criminal prosecutions—for example, in relation to a failure to notify under the Act.

Question: Are there any exclusions?

Answer: Yes. There are both primary exemptions and miscellaneous exemptions. The primary exemptions broadly cover:

(a) the safeguarding of national security;

(b) the prevention or detection of crime and the assessment and collection of taxes;

(c) the physical or mental health of the data subject;

(d) processing of personal data in respect of regulatory functions exercised by public enforcement agencies;

(e) journalistic uses and also artistic and literary purposes;

(f) research purposes;

(g) information made public by law (eg the electoral list), but the exemption only applies in the hands of the person who is required to make it public;

(h) disclosures required by law;

(i) disclosures in connection with legal proceedings;

(j) domestic purposes.

In addition, there are a number of miscellaneous exemptions covering such items as legal professional privilege, corporate finance, management planning and confidential references given by the data controller.

Question: OK, so how do I notify under the Act?

Answer: Forms can be obtained from the Information Commissioner at Wycliffe House, Water Lane,

Wilmslow, Cheshire SK9 5AF (tel: 01625 545 745). Online forms and further details can also be obtained from the Information Commissioner's website: www.ico.gov.uk

At first sight, the forms can look somewhat forbidding, but they are quite easy to complete once one has understood the basic format. One starts by a description of the data subjects; in other words, the types of individuals about whom personal data are to be held. Then one goes on to identify the classes of personal data which are to be held about the data subjects identified previously; and then identify the sources of personal data relating to the data subjects, and to whom disclosures are to be made. Finally, there is a section on overseas transfer of data.

All this is done by means of a series of boxes that need to be ticked and, if one follows the guidance notes, this operation is, as I have said above, much easier than would seem at first sight.

Question: So what happens when I have notified the Information Commissioner?

Answer: First, one has to make sure that the notification is kept up-to-date, and is renewed every three years. Failure to notify, or to keep the notice up-to-date or to renew, would give rise to a criminal offence. Once having notified, one also has to make sure that one's processing of data complies with the eight Data Protection Principles that are set out in Sch 1 to the 1998 Act (see below).

The Data Protection Principles

Question: What are the Data Protection Principles?

Answer: The eight Data Protection Principles as set out in Sch 1 to the 1998 Act are:

(1) Personal data shall be obtained and processed fairly and lawfully.

(2) Personal data shall be obtained only for one or more specified and lawful purposes, and shall not be further processed in any manner incompatible with that purpose or those purposes.

(3) Personal data shall be adequate, relevant and not excessive in relation to the purpose or purposes for which they are processed.

(4) Personal data shall be accurate and, where necessary, kept up-to-date.

(5) Personal data processed for any purpose or purposes shall not be kept for longer than is necessary for that purpose or those purposes.

(6) Personal data shall be processed in accordance with the rights of data subjects under the 1998 Act.

(7) Appropriate technical and organisational measures shall be taken against unauthorised or unlawful processing of personal data and against accidental loss or destruction of, or damage to, personal data.

(8) Personal data shall not be transferred to a country or territory outside the European Economic Area unless that country or territory ensures an adequate level of protection for the rights and freedoms of data subjects in relation to the processing of personal data.

Question: So what happens if I fail to abide by one of these Principles?

Answer: Failure to comply with a Data Protection Principle is not, in itself, a criminal offence, but the Information Commissioner can take action. The Information Commissioner can use an enforcement notice requiring a data controller to take, or refrain from taking, specified steps, or even to stop processing any personal data generally or data of a specified description or for a specified purpose.

Question: Tell me more about enforcement notices.

Answer: In an enforcement notice, the Information Commissioner will set out the Principle or Principles which he believes have been contravened, and the basis for the allegation. It will go on to stipulate the steps which the Information Commissioner requires to be taken, and the relevant time-period. Finally, it will remind the addressee of a right of appeal to the Data Protection Tribunal.

There is also a notice which the Information Commissioner can issue known as an 'information notice'. This notice requires information from the data controller so that the Information Commissioner can decide whether or not the data controller has complied with the Data Protection Principles. An appeal against an information notice can also be made to the Data Protection Tribunal.

Question: Supposing I do not agree with the notice from the Information Commissioner?

Answer: First, one could take the view that the enforcement notice is unfounded, and simply demand that the Information Commissioner brings a prosecution, where the Information Commissioner would have to prove his or her case in the normal way before the criminal courts. However, since the only defences open to the data controller are that he or she has exercised all due diligence to comply, or there is some legal defect in the notice, it is generally an unwise course. More appropriate is to use the right of appeal under the 1998 Act to the Data Protection Tribunal, a course of action which will have been highlighted in the notice. The Tribunal consists of a legally qualified chairman, together with lay members, and was set up to consider appeals against the Information Commissioner's decision, and it can overturn the Information Commissioner's decision or substitute another decision, if it thinks that more appropriate.

Question: When can personal data be disclosed?

Answer: The principal situation in which data can be disclosed is where the disclosure is made in accordance with the Disclosures Section of the data controller's notification entry, and the disclosure is not in breach of the first Data Protection Principle.

However, as we have seen, data can also be disclosed when it is required by law, or needed for an investigation into a potential criminal offence where a failure to disclose would be likely to prejudice the prevention or detection of crime. Disclosures can be made for the purpose of obtaining legal advice or in the course of legal proceedings in which the person making the disclosure is a party or a witness. They can also be made in emergencies where the disclosure is urgently required for preventing injury or other damage to anyone's health. Finally, disclosure is allowed where it is made to employees or agents of the data user and where the disclosure is made with the data subject's consent.

Question: I understand that the first Data Protection Principle, ie that data shall be processed fairly and lawfully, is the most significant one for direct marketing. Is this so?

Answer: Yes, in practice the first Data Protection Principle is the most important one for marketing interests and, in considering whether the Principle has been complied with, the Information Commissioner will take account of all the circumstances of the obtaining, and the method by which the information was obtained. The individual must be aware of the identity of the data controller, the purposes for which personal data are to be held or not, and the disclosures of personal data to third parties. Information is always regarded as having been obtained fairly if it is obtained from a person who is authorised by law to supply it. In other situations, the Information Commissioner will make a judgment by having regard to the method by which the information was obtained, including the question of whether or not any person who provided the information was deceived or misled as to the purpose or purposes for which it was to be held, used or disclosed.

In the case of *Innovations (Mail Order) Ltd v The Data Protection Registrar* [1993], a case heard before the Data Protection Tribunal, it was held that any non-obvious purpose or purposes for which the data is being collected should be made clear to the individual before the information is obtained. The Tribunal said that where information comprised names obtained for a particular purpose, and is subsequently used for another purpose that the data subjects were not told about, the data user must seek the positive consent of the data subjects if use is to be made of their data for that non-obvious purpose.

Question: Tell me more about the *Innovations* case.

Answer: The case related largely to the point at which consumers should be told of an intention by a mail order company to make use of names and addresses for list broking purposes. In this case, 'Innovations' included a note on an acceptance of order form to the effect that they made customer lists available to other companies, and that consumers could avoid further mailings by sending an exact copy of their address label to an address set out on the note.

The Data Protection Registrar, the predecessor of the Information Commissioner concluded that the notice should have been given to the data subject, ie the consumer, before his or her name and address were supplied in connection with the order. The Data Protection Tribunal agreed with the Registrar and made these comments:

'We conclude that a later notice may be a commendable way of providing a further warning, but whether it does so or not, we conclude that the law requires in the circumstance we have here that when possible the warning must be before the obtaining.

This can best be done by including the warning in the advertisement itself. Where it may not be possible (eg the use of existing names for a new purpose) we consider that the obligation to obtain the data subject's positive consent for the non-obvious use of their data falls upon the data user.'

Question: How does one overcome the problem of a non-obvious purpose?

Answer: When personal information is collected, for example, as part of a sales promotion, it is clear that the information can be considered fairly obtained for the fulfilment of that promotion, and the Information Commissioner takes the view that, within reason, it should be obvious to an individual respondent that the data controller might use the personal data for future direct marketing of its own related goods and services. It was, after all, the reason for which the consumer gave their personal data. If, however, there is the intention of using the data for other mailings, or for transfer to third parties, then it is important to have an appropriate statement which informs the consumers that this will happen, and give them the option of saying no.

There is a growing use of data capture in promotions, and sometimes promotional techniques, such as draws, are used solely to incentivise data capture exercises. Normally, this is done by means of what is termed an 'opt-out box'. Something along the following lines is needed:

'From time to time we may pass your details to other companies so that they can write to you about their products or services. If you do not wish to receive such mailings, please tick this box.'

E-mail and text are treated differently—see later in the chapter.

Question: What about sensitive data?

Answer: There are certain pieces of information that are stated to be 'sensitive personal data' and processing of such material is tightly controlled. 'Sensitive data' is defined as information relating to racial or ethnic origin, political opinions, religious or other similar beliefs, membership of a trade union, physical or mental health, sex life and criminal records.

In relation to such data the data subject has to give explicit consent. Processing is also allowed in certain other situations, such as where it is necessary in relation to legal advice, medical purposes and the administration of justice. Regulations also permit the processing of sensitive personal data in relation to ten specific situations, including confidential counselling, insurance and pension payments, protection of the public from crime, political parties and research and archive material.

Question: What about host mailings?

Answer: There are a number of ways in which host mailings can arise in direct marketing—one of the most common being where a mail order trader inserts a third party's leaflet in mailings to its own customers. The Information Commissioner takes the view that, where personal data are used for 'package insert' host mailings and everyone receives the same insert, data users are not generally required to provide a notification. A notification is, however, needed if the host mailing is to be selective or if 'solus' host mailings are to be carried out.

Rights

Question: What rights are individuals given under the 1998 Act?

Answer: Perhaps the most important right is for the data subject to secure access, subject to limited exceptions, to the relevant data, on payment of a modest fee of up to £10. This enables data subjects to know what data is kept in respect of them.

Individuals have the right to prevent processing of personal data for the purposes of direct marketing—a right which we discuss below. Additionally, any person may ask the Information Commissioner to carry out an assessment of whether any processing of personal data has been carried out in compliance with the Act. Where the data subject believes data will be processed in a way that is likely to cause him or her damage or distress, the data subject can serve a 'data subject notice' on the data controller requiring the processing to cease or not to begin. If the data controller takes no action, the data subject can seek a court order.

In addition, a data subject can secure compensation from the courts for damage and associated distress caused by any contravention of the requirements of the 1998 Act entitling them to compensation. The court can also order the rectification, blocking or destruction of any data that has been the subject of a successful claim under this provision.

Finally, an individual may feel that the user of his or her data is in breach of one or more of the eight Data Protection Principles and is entitled to complain to the Information Commissioner who can issue, in appropriate cases, an enforcement notice.

Question: Tell me about the right to prevent direct marketing?

Answer: An individual has the right, under the 1998 Act, to prevent direct marketing. To do this, an individual must send a notice in writing to a data controller asking for the processing of any personal data relating to him or her that is to be used for direct marketing purposes to cease. The data controller must comply, failing which the Information Commissioner can issue an enforcement notice on the basis that the data controller has breached the sixth Data Protection Principle.

Question: So what rights are conferred by The Privacy and Electronic Communications (EC Directive) Regulations 2003?

Answer: These Regulations provide for four basic rights:

(1) Private individuals must not receive direct marketing faxes without positive consent.

(2) There should be no telephone calls to private individuals if they have objected to receiving them.

(3) No direct marketing faxes should be sent to businesses if they have objected to receiving them.

(4) No e-mails or text marketing communications without positive consent.

Question: Tell me more about the position in respect of e-mail when used for direct marketing purposes—does there need to be an opt-in box?

Answer: Under The Privacy and Electronic Communications (EC Directive) Regulations 2003, a data subject must give express consent to the receipt of marketing communications by e-mail or text. That consent could be given by means of a box which must be ticked in order to opt-in to receiving such communications. This is not, however, necessary if it is made clear that by giving their e-mail address or mobile 'phone number, they will then receive future marketing communications. It must, however, be clear. Hiding a statement about future marketing communications within the small print will not suffice. It must be in close proximity to where an e-mail address is to be given. Alternatively, positive consent could be given by asking data subjects to click on an icon.

Question: What happens if they are existing customers?

Answer: You do not need prior consent if you have already obtained the recipients' e-mail or text details in the course of the sale or the negotiations for the sale of a product or service and the proposed marketing communications are in respect of similar products and services. However, every subsequent communication will have to have an opt-out facility. This exception to the normal rule is colloquially known as the 'Soft opt-in'.

Children

Question: Finally, what about data protection and children?

Answer: This is a sensitive area and one can only point to advice from the Information Commissioner. In his guidance, the Information Commissioner endorses the view that personal data must only be collected from children with the explicit and verifiable consent of the child's parent/guardian unless that child is 12 years or over, the information collected is restricted to that necessary to enable the child to be sent further, but limited, online communications and it is clear what is involved.

Additionally, as far as members of the Direct Marketing Association (DMA) are concerned, the DMA Code states:

> 'When collecting data in an online environment from minors under 16 years of age, members must secure consent from that minor's parent or guardian. When collecting data in an offline environment from minors under 14 years of age, members must secure consent from that minor's parent or guardian'.

As far as promotional activity is concerned, it is probably wise to say that parental consent is needed for those under 18. Indeed, such requirements are common in promotional rules and, apart from anything else, they demonstrate on the part of the promoter a socially responsible approach and one that lays marketing to children less open to criticism. Given the considerable opposition to marketing to children particularly in some European countries, that has to be a sensible approach.

CHAPTER 6

INTELLECTUAL PROPERTY

Definitions

Question: What is 'intellectual property'?

Answer: Intellectual property is the name we give to the branch of law that covers copyright, trade marks and patents.

Question: What do we mean by 'copyright'?

Answer: Copyright is essentially a right of the creator of original material to control the reproduction of that material for as long as the material stays within copyright. Copyright exists basically in every original piece of literary, artistic, dramatic or musical work, and in sound recordings, films, television broadcasts, cable programmes and published editions.

Question: What is *not* subject to copyright protection?

Answer: The main exception to copyright protection is in respect of ideas and concepts. Although the tangible expression of an idea will be copyright, the idea itself is not copyright—although it may be protected in other ways, as we shall see later.

   Another important exclusion from copyright protection relates to names, titles and slogans. In a well-known case early in the last century, no copyright was held to subsist in the slogan 'Beauty is a social necessity, not a luxury'. (*Sinanide v La Maison Kosmeo* [1928])

   However, it is interesting to note that copyright does exist in such items as train timetables and football fixture lists, not so much on the basis of the originality of the information, but on the basis of the work involved in gathering and presenting the material. Such documents are held to be compilations and the legislation specifically provides that they are subject to copyright protection as literary works.

Ownership of copyright

Question: Who owns the copyright and for how long?

Answer: The copyright belongs to the author of the copyright work, with the one exception that in the case of work created by employees in the course of their employment, the copyright belongs to their employer unless otherwise agreed. So, with work created in-house by employees of an advertising agency or sales promotion consultancy, the copyright would belong to the agency—but not work created by freelancers. The author of a work is normally the person who created it, though the rules are different for films and sound recordings.

Copyright in literary, artistic, dramatic or musical works currently lasts for life of the author plus 70 years from the end of the calendar year in which the author dies.

Question: How do you copyright something?

Answer: It is a widely held belief that one can go through some process of registration and thereby 'copyright' a piece of work. However, in the UK there is no process of registration that needs to be undertaken because copyright protection arises automatically once a piece of work has been created to which copyright protection applies.

Question: I understand there are regulations on databases?

Answer: Yes. The Copyright and Rights in Databases Regulations 1997 provide that there is a copyright to protect the structure of a database so long as the database contents satisfy an 'intellectual creativity' test.

Separately, there is a database right to protect substantial work in obtaining, verifying or presenting the database contents. The right lasts for 15 years.

The impact of these regulations was thoroughly considered in the case of *British Horseracing Board v William Hill* in 2004—a case which involved a reference to the European Court of Justice.

Ideas and concepts

Question: The most valuable part of a promotion is often the idea or concept. Are you really saying that this cannot be protected?

Answer: As we have already seen, there is no copyright in an idea or concept, so copyright protection cannot be used to protect a creative idea. However, that does not mean that the idea is not capable of some protection by using other legal devices. The main way this can be done is by invoking what is known as the 'law of confidentiality'. The law requires the following aspects to be present:

(a)   The circumstances in which the information was communicated import an obligation of confidence, in particular by making it clear to the other party that the material is copyright.

(b)   The content of the idea is a clearly identifiable original, of potential commercial attractiveness and capable of reaching fruition.

This was well illustrated by what has become known as the *Rock Follies* case (*Fraser v Thames Television* [1983]). Three members of the pop group Rock Bottom went to Thames Television and outlined their ideas for a new television series. They did so in circumstances which made it clear that the ideas were being communicated in confidence and this was also tied-up in a contract by which Thames paid £500 for an option. Thames Television at that stage said they were not interested in the idea and three years later a series was run by Thames Television based on the idea which had been presented to them. Since the ideas and concepts had been presented in circumstances which imposed a duty of confidentiality on Thames Television, the suit against them was successful and the three individuals were awarded damages of £500,000.

Question: What if the idea is commonplace?

Answer: There is an old saying, 'you can't make a silk purse out of a sow's ear'. In this context, it means you cannot make a promotional idea or concept confidential if it is very much public property. So the idea of an instant win promotion could not be made confidential, unless the proposed use was highly innovative or presented in a very original way.

Moral rights

Question: I have heard about 'moral rights'—what are they?

Answer: Moral rights belong to the author of a copyright literary, dramatic, musical or artistic work and to the director of a copyright film. Under the Copyright, Designs and Patents Act 1988, such rights cannot be assigned to anyone else, because they are personal rights. They can, however, be waived. So what are those moral rights?

(1) *The right to be identified as author or director.* The right does not apply unless it has been asserted, either generally or specifically in relation to a particular use of the material. Such an assertion must be in writing, signed by the author or director or contained in a document which assigns the copyright.

There are a number of exceptions to this right, the most important of which, for agencies, is where use is made of copyright material by the copyright owner or with his or her consent, and where the copyright belongs to the author's or director's employer. In an agency situation, this would mean no moral rights would apply to employees and their work, provided that any usage was by the agency or with the agency's consent. Again, this would not include freelancers, and in their case agencies need to think about waivers of moral rights.

(2) *The right to object to derogatory treatment of work.* The law provides that an author or film director has the right not to have his or her work subjected to derogatory treatment. What does this mean?

    (a) 'Treatment' means any addition to, deletion from or alteration to, or adaptation of the work, other than a translation of a literary or dramatic work, or an arrangement or transcription of a musical work involving no more than a change of key or register.

    (b) 'Derogatory' means any treatment which amounts to distortion or mutilation of the work, or is otherwise prejudicial to the honour or reputation of the author or director.

The right to object to derogatory treatment of work will not apply to employees unless they were identified at the time of the derogatory treatment or were previously identified in or on published copies of the work.

Practical issues

Question: What must I consider in relation to copyright?

Answer: First, you must remember that most creative material will be copyright and, except for material created in-house in the course of employment, it will be necessary to make sure that the necessary assignments or usage licences are obtained. Also, you must remember to secure waivers of moral rights in respect of externally commissioned creative work.

Secondly, you need to protect your own creative material. As I have said, material is either subject to copyright protection or it is not. However, there are certain steps that one can take to reinforce one's claim to ownership of the copyright. It is important to keep copies of original drawings and other original creative material, in order to be ready for any challenge on ownership. It is also advisable to consider putting a 'C' in a circle and the word 'Copyright' against it and perhaps the name of the copyright owner and the date; this should be used as a way of indicating that a particular piece of material is copyright and to act as something of a warning that the copyright owner will be likely to protect their interests.

Trade marks

Question: Where do trade marks fit in?

Answer: Under the Trade Marks Act 1994 (the 1994 Act), registration is possible for 'any sign capable of being represented graphically which is capable of distinguishing goods or services of one undertaking from those of other undertakings'.

The possibilities for registration under the 1994 Act are extensive.

Under the 1994 Act, the following are registerable: sounds, shapes, slogans and smells. Slogans will only be registered where they can be shown to be distinctive. Most slogans are not distinctive and never will be because they are, to coin a phrase, 'here today, gone tomorrow'. And one should remember that it is no use going through the time and expense of an application for trade mark registration if the likelihood is that a new slogan will be in use by the time the procedural formalities have been completed.

The 1994 Act has a provision which allows unauthorised use of a registered trade mark where it is used for identification purposes, so long as it is in accordance with honest industrial and commercial practices. This is a provision designed to facilitate comparative advertising.

Question: Do we have any decisions from the courts on when the use of trade marks for identifying the goods of another trader is to be regarded as acceptable?

Answer: A series of cases have thrown up robust decisions from the courts. In *Barclays Bank Plc v RBS Advanta [1996]*, Barclays Bank attempted to stop a comparative advertisement relating to credit cards and interest rates. The court took the view that the facts as stated were correct, the advertisement was not misleading to the people to whom it was addressed, and therefore the use of the trade mark was in accordance with honest industrial practices.

In the case of *Vodafone Group Plc v Orange Personal Communications Services Ltd [1997]*, the claimant sued over the use of their trade mark in an advertisement which claimed that Orange users saved £20 over Vodafone's tariffs. The court concluded that the comparison was a fair one and not misleading. The trade mark infringement claim therefore failed.

Accordingly, one can say with some confidence that the use of other companies' trade marks will be allowed unless it is in the context of an unfair and misleading advertisement.

Question: When can trade marks be used?

Answer: (a)   The most obvious circumstance in which a registered trade mark can be used is where there is permission or authority to use the mark. Sometimes that will be express permission, although there are many circumstances in which there is implied consent. For example, if the purpose of a promotion is to promote the sales of the goods which have the mark on them, then it is reasonable to assume that there is implied permission for that exposure and use of the mark because it is necessary to assist in the marketing of the relevant goods.

(b) As we have seen already, a trade mark can be used to identify the goods or services of another, but it must be in accordance with honest industrial or commercial practices. If not, the use will be treated as infringing the trade mark if the use takes unfair advantage of, or is detrimental to, the distinctive character or repute of the mark.

Question: How can I check out trade marks?

Answer: If there is any doubt about whether a mark is registered, then the easiest course is to go online to the Patents Office website (www.patent.gov.uk) and do a search. Alternatively, one can ask a trade mark agent to conduct a search and prepare a report. The existence of an 'R' in a circle will indicate a registered mark—to use such a device when a mark is not registered is a criminal offence. Sometimes, one will see the letters 'TM' in a circle. This indicates an unregistered or common law trade mark. As long as there is no confusion, there is little the owner of an unregistered trade mark can do to stop unauthorised use.

Question: What are the consequences of an infringement of copyright or registered trade mark?

Answer: Damages are possible as compensation for an infringement of copyright or a registered trade mark although, if the damage suffered is relatively slight in commercial terms, it is unlikely that the amount of damages that a court would award would make it worthwhile pursuing a case to full trial. In most cases, the only remedy worth having for an infringement of copyright or a registered trade mark is an injunction, which puts an end to the relevant infringement. An application for an injunction can be made before a full trial but, if the application for an injunction is unsuccessful, in most cases the matter does not proceed to a full hearing.

Patents

Question: What are patents?

Answer: Patents were first granted in the reign of Elizabeth
                   I to facilitate the growth of new industries. Patents
                   encourage industrial innovation by giving the inventor
                   of an industrial technique a monopoly right to exploit
                   that invention for a period of 20 years—after which
                   the invention is considered to be in the public domain.

                   However, patent protection does not protect innova-
                   tive design but only the essential function.

Question: When do patents become relevant?

Answer: 1. In relation to the production of promotional mer-
                      chandise, it is important to make sure that no
                      existing patents are infringed. This is particularly
                      important given the widespread importation of
                      promotional merchandise from countries in the
                      Far East, such as China and Korea.

                   2. Occasionally, in developing a new promotional
                      technique or developing a novel way of presenting
                      an existing promotional technique, a device is
                      produced which is patentable. One example that
                      has come my way over the years is related to a
                      drinks can with a device that enabled money to
                      pop out when winning cans were opened. This
                      was an invention, and an application was made
                      to patent this device. This does not happen very
                      often, but sales promotion practitioners should be
                      aware of the possibility.

CHAPTER 7

PRICE PROMOTIONS AND PRICE CLAIMS

Introduction

Question: Where is the law on price claims to be found?

Answer: The law relating to price promotions is mainly contained in Pt III of the Consumer Protection Act 1987 (the 1987 Act). Section 20 of the 1987 Act prohibits the giving, by any means, in the course of a business an indication which is misleading as to the price at which any goods, services, accommodation or facilities are available. This offence is very widely based, as the following examples will reveal.

     Guidance as to what is or is not misleading is given in the Code of Practice for Traders on Price Indications recently re-issued by the Department of Trade and Industry (the Prices Code) (reproduced in Appendix 2 below). This Prices Code enjoys a unique status in law: Its recommendations are not mandatory, by which we mean that a price indication not covered by the Prices Code would not of itself be misleading and therefore unlawful. However, compliance with the Prices Code would constitute a defence of 'all due diligence and all reasonable precautions' as provided by s 39(1) of the 1987 Act. Furthermore, a court may have regard to the recommendations in the Prices Code in determining whether or not a particular price indication is unlawful.

Indications that a price is less than it actually is

Question: We have often heard of self-service retailers being prosecuted for selling goods at a higher price than indicated. Is that an offence and can it affect goods subject to promotions?

Answer: The offence of charging a higher price at the check-out than appears on the goods or on a shelf-edge marker is one of the oldest pricing problems for retailers. It is known in the trade as 'buncing'. It was first prohibited by the Trade Descriptions Act 1968 and since then many retailers have fallen foul of it. Rarely is it done deliberately; most often it is simply carelessness in failing to alter marked prices or bar Prices Codes on old stock when prices are increased.

Section 21 of the 1987 Act, which gives guidance in respect of the term 'misleading' in s 20, states that a price is misleading if it indicates that the price is less than it in fact is. Indeed, the present law is even wider in its application than the old one, for it stipulates that a price indication can become misleading after it is given; the offence is committed if some or all consumers might reasonably be expected to rely on the price indication after it is given and the person who gives the indication fails to take all such steps as are reasonable to prevent consumers from relying on the indication.

The indicated price for goods which are offered in promotions can also be caught by this offence.

Question: How can incentive goods be caught by the suggestion that the price is less than it actually is?

Answer: It is most likely to arise where prices have changed immediately before or after a promotion with stock of the promoted goods remaining on display simul-taneously with standard non-promoted packs. It is basically a question of controlled stock rotation.

Reductions from a previous price

Question: How can genuine reductions in prices be indicated?

Answer: This is the most straightforward of all price comparisons, provided it complies with the following basic
rules:

(a) the higher and the reduced price must be shown;

(b) the higher price must be the last price at which the
goods were offered in the previous six months;

(c) the product should have been available to consumers at the higher price for at least 28 days in
the preceding six months*;

(d) the previous price should have been offered for
that period at the same shop where the reduced
price is now being offered.

* *Note:* The 28-day rule does not apply to food and
drink or non-food perishables if they have a shelf life
of less than six weeks.

For full guidance as to reduced prices, see s 1.2 of the
Prices Code (in Appendix 2 below).

Question: If it is impossible to satisfy these rules, can a disclaimer
be used?

Answer: To avoid committing an offence, positive statements
rather than disclaimers are required in order that price
comparisons be fair and reasonable.

Question: (a) What positive statement would suffice if the 28-
day rule had not been complied with?

(b) What positive statement would suffice if the
goods had not been previously offered at the
higher price in the same shop?

Answer: (a) The actual period during which the higher price
had been on offer should be stated, eg 'SALE:
£25—Previous price £30—Offered from 1 to 15
December'.*

(b) An indication of the shops where they had been
offered is required, eg 'These goods were on sale
at the higher price in our five largest stores'.*

* Note: These examples of positive statements would not be acceptable in all cases. If, to take an extreme case, a higher price had only been on offer for a very short period indeed (say, one hour), the price indication may be misleading even though a positive statement had been made. The same might be the case if a very large multiple company with 300 stores had offered the goods at the higher price in only one or two of those stores. In all cases the comparison must be fair and reasonable, notwithstanding the use of positive statements.

Question: How do these rules apply to catalogue or mail order traders?

Answer: Any comparison with a previous price should be with the price in the trader's own last issued catalogue, advertisement or leaflet. If the product is offered in both catalogues etc and shops, the higher price should be the last price at which the goods were offered. In all other respects the rules given above apply.

Question: Can we offer a series of reductions on the same goods?

Answer: Yes. The Prices Code makes allowance for circumstances where it is wished to make further reductions during the same sale or special-offer period. Only the highest price need comply with the 28-day rule. See para 1.2.6 of the Prices Code (in Appendix 2 below).

Question: Are there any restrictions as to how a genuine previous price must be indicated?

Answer: The expressions used must be clear. Thus 'normal price', 'regular price' or 'usual price' should not be used alone. They should be qualified to show that they are the seller's own previous price, eg 'our normal price'.

Question: I understand there has been a recent case involving the Officer's Club in which previous prices was an issue. What does it tell us?

Answer: In this case, the retailer's own price discount advertisements took the general form of '70 per cent off everything'. The court found that the advertisements were misleading as the higher prices used for the basis of the comparison were not, in the Court's opinion, genuine higher prices. As a result of this case, the Office of Fair Trading (OFT) has advised that to be genuine a higher price must satisfy the following criteria:

• The seller must honestly believe that the price is an appropriate sale price for the goods. In other words, he must honestly believe that the goods could be sold in significant numbers at that price.

• The seller must have placed a significant quantity of the goods on sale at the higher price. In this context, a significant quantity for sale at the higher price involves a snapshot comparison at a particular moment in time between what had previously been offered for sale at the higher price and what at that later snapshot moment was offered for sale at the discounted price.

• The goods must be offered for sale at the higher price for a period at least sufficient to be a genuine offer of sale to the section of the public likely to be interested in purchasing such goods, that is, sufficient time for knowledge of the availability of the goods to be acquired by that section of the public, and sufficient time for them to view the goods, make up their minds whether to purchase them, and, if so, to complete the purchase of them.

'Significant quantity' and 'Sufficient time' are not defined but the OFT says that this will allow retailers, regulators and the courts to apply a commonsense judgment.

Recommended prices

Question: Can we compare our selling prices with genuine manufacturers' recommended prices?

Answer: Yes, provided you comply with the following rules:

(a) Initials or abbreviations may not be used except for 'RRP' to describe a recommended retail price and 'man rec price' to indicate a manufacturer's recommended price. In all other cases the basis of the comparison with a recommended price must be spelt out in full.

(b) The recommended price must have been recommended to the retailer by the manufacturer or supplier as a price at which the product might be sold to consumers.

(c) The retailer must deal with the manufacturer or supplier on normal commercial terms.

(d) The recommended price is not significantly higher than prices at which the product is generally sold at the time the comparison is first made.

Question: How can we judge whether a recommended price is not significantly higher than prices at which the product is generally sold?

Answer: Commonsense is the best guide to what is a reasonable recommended price, particularly when supported by a survey of prices charged for comparable goods.

It is the retailer's responsibility to consider whether a recommended price is consistent with prices generally being offered for the goods concerned, but it should be pointed out that the offence in s 20 of the 1987 Act can be committed by any company giving misleading indications of price to consumers.

Question: What is the difference between a 'recommended price' and 'resale price maintenance'?

Answer: Resale price maintenance occurs when a manufacturer or supplier seeks to compel retailers to sell goods supplied to them at a minimum price. The Resale Prices Act 1976, as amended, makes such practices unlawful. Whenever a manufacturer or supplier wishes to recommend retail selling prices it must make it clear that it is merely a recommendation and not a minimum price.

Question: It is often the case that manufacturers print a selling price on packs. How can a retailer sell below that price if he does not wish to obliterate it from the pack?

Answer: The Prices Code recognises this problem and provides that such printed prices may be regarded as recommended prices by the retailer without the need to indicate that they are recommended prices. The retailer is therefore free to offer the goods at a lower price and to mark that lower price on the packs without first obliterating the manufacturer's marked price. This does not apply to retailers' own-label packs.

Question: Are there any bans on RRPs?

Answer: The Restrictions on Agreements and Conduct (Specified Domestic Electrical Goods) Order 1998 prohibits suppliers from notifying RRPs to dealers in respect of camcorders, dishwashers, freezers, fridges, hi-fi systems, tumble dryers, televisions, video cassette recorders and washing machines. For Prices Code requirements as to recommended prices, see paras 1.6 and 1.7 thereof (in Appendix 2 below).

Introductory offers

Question: Introductory offers are important for the launching of new products or businesses. What are the rules?

Answer: A promotion must not be called an introductory offer unless it is the intention to continue to offer the product for sale after the offer period is over and at a higher price. The offer must have a reasonably short life or it could become misleading to call it an introductory offer. The period may vary depending on the nature of the product and its shelf life. It is, however, very unlikely that an offer would be deemed to be misleading if an expiry date is given and the price which will pertain after that date is quoted.

However, the Prices Code suggests that an after-promotion price should only be given if the trader is certain that, subject only to circumstances beyond its control, identical products will continue to be offered at the higher price for at least 28 days in the three months after the end of the offer period or after the offer stocks run out. This suggestion has been criticised because the purpose of many introductory offers is to test public response to a new product and if demand is heavy it may be impossible to honour the 28-day period. It must be assumed, until a court rules otherwise, that heavy and unexpected demand would be deemed to be circumstances beyond control.

Question: If demand is lower than expected may an introductory offer be extended?

Answer: Yes. The Prices Code requires a positive statement such as 'Extended for a further two weeks until 1 June' to make it clear that the period has been extended.

For the suggestions as to introductory offers, see para 1.3 of the Prices Code (in Appendix 2 below).

Question: Can we avoid the rules on introductory offers by calling the offer an 'after-promotion price'?

Answer: No, the rules are the same for both types of promotion. It is also necessary to state in full what is meant whenever future prices are quoted, ie 'after-sale price' not 'ASP' and 'after-promotion price' not 'APP'.

Comparisons with other traders' prices

Question: Can comparisons be made with other traders' prices?

Answer: The government recognises that competition in the market is beneficial to consumers and it is there-fore necessary to permit fair comparisons with other traders' prices. The Prices Code, however, makes it difficult to do so without risking the commission of an offence. The rules are:

(a) The quoted 'other trader's price' must be accurate and up-to-date. This is nearly impossible to achieve because as soon as the other trader learns of the comparison it is likely to reduce its price, thereby making the comparison misleading.

(b) The name of the other trader must be clearly and prominently stated with the price comparison.

(c) The shop where the other trader's price applies must be identified if the other trader is in fact trading from a shop.

(d) The other trader's price must relate to the same products or substantially similar products. Any differences between the products must be stated clearly.

Question: Can general statements about prices charged by other traders be made?

Answer: The Prices Code refers to price promise statements such as 'If you can buy this product elsewhere for less, we will refund the difference', and requires that such statements should not be made in relation to 'own-brand' products which other traders do not stock unless the offer will also apply to other traders' equivalent goods. Further, if there are any conditions attached to such offers they must be clearly stated.

Comparisons with other traders' prices are always difficult and, to some extent, dangerous. They are more likely to succeed in relation to mail order offers where the other traders' prices are quoted in a catalogue and cannot be easily changed.

Question: Are there any other problems with comparisons with other traders' prices?

Answer: If another trader's price is incorrectly stated, not only would the trader making the comparison face the possibility of criminal proceedings under Pt III of the 1987 Act but the offended trader may sue for damages for loss of business. It is a technique that should be used with the greatest care.

'Basket of goods' comparisons can create problems where one retailer compares a range of its goods with those of another retailer. In such cases, it is important to make sure that one is comparing like with like. It is also important to make it clear when the comparison was made. Prices change quickly and the comparison needs to be presented as a snapshot in time. Guidance on 'basket of goods' comparisons can be obtained from the Committee of Advertising Practice Copy Advice Service.

References to value or worth

Question: What about general statements concerning the value or worth of goods offered?

Answer: The Prices Code prohibits comparisons of selling prices with amounts described only as 'worth' or 'value'. General advertising slogans and statements about general trading practice, such as 'Low prices is our policy', or innocuous statements such as 'Unbeatable value' or 'The greatest value in town' are considered to be advertisers' puffery and are not seen as price claims.

The test to be considered in each case is whether the slogan or words used are likely to suggest a comparison with another price in the minds of consumers. All price comparisons should be capable of substantiation.

Sales and special events

Question: In a 'sale' is it necessary that all goods offered should have been previously offered at a higher price?

Answer: There is nothing to prevent reduced goods being sold side-by-side with other goods which have not been reduced or further goods which have been brought in specially for the sale, provided that each group of goods is clearly identified. Goods which have been reduced should be marked with the original higher price; the reduced price; and be distinguished from other goods which have not been reduced. Merchandise being sold at its normal price should be separately displayed so that there can be no doubt that it is not a part of the sale. Goods brought in for the event should be marked 'special purchase' or something similar, and should not be double priced.

Question: Is it in order to use general price statements such as 'half-marked price'?

Answer: Yes, provided you also indicate the higher and lower prices on each item of merchandise and take care that all reductions are in fact at least 50 per cent.

Question: What about statements such as 'up to 50 per cent off'?

Answer: The Prices Code requires that at least 10 per cent of the range of products on offer should have been reduced by 50 per cent. For sales and special events, see para 1.9 of the Prices Code (in Appendix 2 below).

Price comparisons in different circumstances

Question: Is it still permitted to quote different prices for different quantities of goods?

Answer: Yes. You can offer, for example, '£1 each, 4 for £3.50'.

Question: What about different prices for goods in different condition?

Answer: It is acceptable to quote 'Seconds £20, when perfect £ 30' etc. The 'when perfect' price should have been previously charged by the trader concerned and the 28-day rule and the rules as to different shops should be followed. If the 'when perfect' price is a recommended price, then the rules on recommended prices should be followed and, if it is another trader's price, then the rules on comparisons with other traders' prices should be followed.

Question: Can different prices be charged depending on the availability of the goods?

Answer: It is in order to quote different prices such as 'Price £50—when specially ordered £60'. The test is whether the different circumstances are clearly stated.

Question: What are the rules for different prices for goods in a different state?

Answer: This usually applies to goods available both in kit-form and ready-assembled form. The rules are that it is in order to quote 'Price in kit-form £50, price ready-assembled £70', but the Prices Code suggests that a third of the total stock should be in the different state, eg one-third ready assembled and two-thirds in kit-form, or vice versa, in the same shop. If another trader's price for one or other of the different states is being used as a basis for comparison, then the rules on comparisons with other traders' prices should be followed.

Question: Is it still in order to quote different prices for different groups of people?

Answer: Yes, this is another principle which has not been changed. It is in order to quote, for example, 'Senior citizens' price £2.50—others £5'. The Prices Code, however, gives further advice by stating that words such as 'our normal price' or 'our regular price' should not be used to describe the higher price unless it applies to at least half of the trader's customers.

For Prices Code requirements as to different circumstances see s 1.4 (in Appendix 2 below).

Post, packing and ancillary charges

Question: Must prices quoted to consumers always include postage, packing and other ancillary charges?

Answer: Yes. The Prices Code is quite specific about this and it applies to mail order traders and shops which offer a delivery service. See paras 2.2.4 and 2.2.5 of the Prices Code (in Appendix 2 below). The Price Marking Order 2004 requires prices to be all-inclusive of non-optional ancillary charges, or for their cost to be clearly shown.

VAT

Question: Do the same rules apply to VAT-inclusive prices?

Answer: Where transactions with consumers are concerned, all quoted prices should be VAT-inclusive. For business contracts see para 2.2.8 of the Prices Code (in Appendix 2 below). If rates of VAT should change, the correct VAT-inclusive price should be communicated to consumers before they are committed to a purchase. As with ancillary charges, the Price Marking Order 2004 requires consumer prices to be shown inclusive of VAT and other taxes.

Mail order trade

Question: How long do prices in mail order catalogues remain current?

Answer: The 1987 Act and the Prices Code are quite specific that prices which are correct at the time they are given can become misleading later and thus constitute an offence. This applies if consumers could reasonably be expected still to be relying on prices quoted in catalogues and the mail order trader had not taken all reasonable steps to prevent them from doing so.

Consequently, if prices stated in a current catalogue have to be changed, the very least which should be done is to ensure that anyone who orders goods at the old price is advised of the new price before being committed to the purchase. See s 3.1 of the Prices Code (in Appendix 2 below).

Newspaper and magazine advertisements

Question: For how long are prices quoted in newspaper and magazine advertisements expected to remain current?

Answer: The Prices Code suggests that the period should be a reasonable one and generally not less than seven days. Much would depend on the frequency of publication and whether any indication of possible changes in price was given in the advertisement. See s 3.2 of the Prices Code (in Appendix 2 below).

Method of payment

Question: What is the position with prices when people pay with credit cards?

Answer: A trader does not have to charge the same price to cash and credit card customers. However, if the price varies depending on the method of payment, the Price Indications (Method of Payment) Regulations 1991 require that a clear explanatory statement be given.

Vouchers and coupons

Question: What are the rules about offering vouchers or coupons as an alternative to price promotions?

Answer: The offer of vouchers, coupons, container attachments etc is a useful alternative to direct reductions in price or comparisons with other prices. It is only in certain very unlikely circumstances that there could be a breach of criminal law in relation to a coupon etc promotion. For example, if a collection of a number of bottle-tops were offered as a discount against the price of a further purchase of the product and that discount was not honoured, it could be argued that there was an offence against s 20 of the 1987 Act in that there was a misleading indication of the price to be paid for the further purchase. To the best of my knowledge, there has never been such a case but it is possible that such an offence could be committed.

In all other respects the offer of coupons etc is free from statutory control under Pt III of the 1987 Act because it does not relate to an indication of price. However, regard must be had to the provisions of the British Code of Advertising, Sales Promotion and Direct Marketing which require that the following should be easily seen and understood by consumers:

(a) the method of making use of the opportunity presented by the sales promotion, or of obtaining the goods, services, facilities or refunds on offer;

(b) the nature and number of any proofs of purchase required; and

(c) the cost and conditions of participation in the promotion, including methods of payment and amounts of any additional postage or delivery charges.

Any instructions as to how a consumer may participate in a sales promotion should give the full name of the promoter and the address at which it can be contacted during normal business hours. When such instructions require participants to detach and return a response coupon, the address of the promoter should appear in the material which can be retained by the participant.

There are notes for guidance on best practice in respect of coupons from the Institute of Sales Promotion and endorsed by all the key organisations concerned with the creation and use of coupons. These notes for guidance are set out as Appendix 3 below.

Note: As a consequence of implementing the EU Unfair Commercial Practices Directive, the Government will repeal Pt III of the 1987 Act as the Government regards the proposed legislation as covering the area of law presently contained in Pt III. As a result of this change, the Prices Code will cease to have a role to play as a statutory code of practice, but the Government's intention is to maintain the Code as non-statutory guidance.

CHAPTER 8

FREE AND EXTRA VALUE INCENTIVES

This chapter deals with the offer of free additional goods or services and extra value offers, such as additional quantity in the pack.

Free offers

Question: If goods or services are offered 'free' does this mean that they must be wholly free or can minor ancillary charges, such as postage and packing, be made?

Answer: The unqualified use of the word 'free' in a promotion means that there can be no charges of any kind. The British Code of Advertising, Sales Promotion and Direct Marketing (the CAP Code) requires that offers should not be described as free if there is any direct cost to the consumer, other than a charge not exceeding, as appropriate:

- the minimum, unavoidable cost of responding to the promotion, eg the current public rates of postage, the cost of telephoning up to and including the national rate or the minimum, unavoidable cost of sending an e-mail or SMS text message;

- the true cost of freight or delivery;

- the cost, including incidental expenses, of any travel involved if the consumer collects the goods on offer.

In all cases, the consumer's liability for such costs should be made clear, and there should be no additional charges for packing or handling. For full details of the requirements in the (CAP Code) as to free offers, see cl 32 of the Code (Appendix 1).

Misleading statements about free offers may also be unlawful under s 20 of the Consumer Protection Act 1987 (the 1987 Act). The Code of Practice for Traders on Price Indications (the Prices Code) (see Chapter 7) requires that consumers should be told exactly what they must buy to get the free offer.

Question: Is it necessary to be specific about the finish dates for free offers?

Answer: Yes. The date on which free offers end should always be stated clearly in advertising material.

Question: The offer of free goods sometimes involves fitting before the free goods can be used by consumers. How can misunderstandings about this be prevented?

Answer: By making it absolutely clear in the promotional material what is offered. A statement such as 'Special offer—windows fitted free' leaves the consumer in doubt as to whether the whole deal, ie windows and fitting, are free, or whether it is intended to offer free fitting only. If words such as 'Windows purchased during our special offer period will be fitted free' had been used, the problem would not arise.

Question: Sometimes goods are of a type which are rarely fitted by consumers themselves. Is it still necessary to make it clear that a free offer applies only where fitting is carried out?

Answer: Of course. The Advertising Standards Authority (ASA) has upheld complaints on this very point. In one case a buyer who responded to an advertisement stating 'Free offer—gas effect fire or equivalent fire-side items if you buy a design fireplace now' was refused the gas effect fire on the grounds that it only applied where the fireplace was fitted by the advertiser. The ASA upheld the complaint because the offer was not sufficiently specific. If the words 'fitted by us' had been added to the offer, all would have been well. Such matters are also caught by s 21(1)(b) of the 1987 Act.

Question: Are there any other problematic areas in regard to free incentives?

Answer:	One phenomenon has been the offer of such things as free travel and accommodation in relation to time-share business; free wine with meals at selected restaurants; free allocations of petrol with new cars; and free audio and video cassettes by different performers. By their very nature, such promotions tend to be rather complex and require very careful drafting to ensure that each feature of the offer is easily understood by consumers. The offer of free travel and accommodation is now also subject to the Package Travel, Package Holidays and Package Tour Regulations 1992.
Question:	Can the problems associated with free offers be overcome by calling them 'gifts'?
Answer:	No. A gift is not a gift if it involves any payment, and the rules explained above should be adhered to.
Question:	Can a value be ascribed to free goods, such as 'A valuable set of wine glasses worth £40, free when you buy a case of Nuit St Georges'?
Answer:	No. The Price Indications Code ([1.10.2]—see Appendix 2) requires that where any value is ascribed to a free offer it must be done as if the free offer were itself being sold. By this it is meant that the trader would have to state its usual selling price for the free goods, a recommended price or another trader's price etc. Unsupportable references to 'worth' or 'value' would be unlawful.

Extra value packs

Question:	What are the rules about adding additional quantities to a standard pack of a product, and flashing '10 per cent extra'?
Answer:	This is entirely in order, provided that the additional quantity is included in the declaration of contents, if required. The additional quantity could also be

indicated by a band around the top of the container which fairly represents 10 per cent of the capacity of the standard pack.

Question: You refer to declarations of quantity above as being necessary 'if required'. Are such declarations not necessary on all packaged goods?

Answer: Regulations made under the Weights and Measures Act 1985 (the 1985 Act) provide that certain classes of goods must be marked with a statement of quantity, either by weight, volume, capacity, measurement, length or number, whilst others may be so marked if required. Yet, other goods are wholly exempted from such declarations or are partially so when packed with other goods or in multiple packs. If goods are marked with a declaration of quantity either because they must be or because the packer wishes to do so, that declaration must be for the net contents of the pack including the additional quantity. The presence of the additional quantity could be declared separately in addition to the statutory declaration, eg '250g + 25g—now 275g'.

Question: Are there any additional considerations if we wish to claim that the extra quantity is free?

Answer: It is necessary to ensure that there has been no recent increase in the price of the standard pack immediately before or coincidental with the introduction of the extra quantity pack so that an allegation that the price has been increased to pay for the additional quantity cannot be made. The extra quantity pack should be offered by each retailer at the same price as the standard pack and ideally that price should have prevailed for a continuous period of at least 28 days before the introduction of the extra quantity pack.

Question: What are the problems about offering extra quantity in products subject to prescribed pack ranges?

Answer: Where a product is required to be made up in prescribed pack sizes there is a danger that a pack with a certain amount extra may not fall into the next highest prescribed pack size. For example, biscuits are required to be made up in quantities of 100g, 125g, 150g, 200g, 250g, 300g or a multiple of 100g up to 5kg; packs of 85g or less are exempted. If it was decided to offer 10 per cent extra on a 250g pack, for example, the new pack would be 275g and that is not a permitted pack size. The pack would thus be unlawful. The only alternatives are to pack to the next prescribed size above the standard pack, ie 300g in the example given, thus offering 20 per cent extra, or to offer a small pack of 25g banded to the standard pack, thus keeping the extra quantity to the desired 10 per cent.

Question: Which products are subject to prescribed pack sizes?

Answer: Mainly foodstuffs, including these product categories: barley, rice and similar cereals, certain biscuits, bread, cereal breakfast foods, chocolate products, cocoa products, coffee and coffee mixtures, dried fruits, dried vegetables, edible fats, flour, honey, jams and similar products, jelly preserves, milk, molasses, syrup and treacle, oat products, pasta, potatoes, salt, sugar and tea.

It is recommended that professional advice be sought on all extra quantity promotions for products subject to prescribed pack sizes.

Multiple packs

Question: Are there any problems with the 'Get one extra free' or 'Three for the price of two', etc type of promotion with packs banded together?

Answer: The advice above about recent price increases should be observed. In multiple packs the compulsory labelling requirements of regulations made under the 1985 Act and/or the Food Safety Act 1990 should be borne in mind.

For food products it is necessary that the product name, the list of ingredients, the minimum durability date, the name and address of the packer or seller, the indication of origin and instructions for use or storage if required and the statement of quantity must be clearly visible. For non-foods the basic requirement is the statement of quantity but there are special additional labelling requirements in relation to cosmetics, medicinal products and certain dangerous products.

If all of the information required by law can be seen through the banding, all is well. If it cannot, then the information must be repeated on the banding or outer packaging. In most cases, it will be necessary to give an overall statement of quantity, eg '5 × 250g', in addition to the weight marking of '250g' on each individual pack.

CHAPTER 9

BRIBERY AND CORRUPTION

Bribery legislation

Question: What legislation covers this field?

Answer: The Public Bodies Corrupt Practices Act 1889 (the 1889 Act) and the Prevention of Corruption Acts 1906–1916.

Section 1 of the 1889 Act makes it an offence where any person, unaccompanied or with others:

(1) corruptly solicits or receives or agrees to receive any gift, loan, fee, reward or advantage whatever as an inducement or reward for, or otherwise on account of, any member of a public body or public official or decides not to do something in respect of any matter or transaction with which the relevant public body is concerned;

(2) corruptly gives, promises, or offers any gift, loan, fee, reward or advantage as an inducement or reward for or otherwise on account of any member of a public body or any public official for doing something or deciding not to do something in respect of any matter or transaction with which the relevant public body is concerned.

Subsection 1(1) basically covers the corrupt acceptance of gifts. Subsection 1(2) covers the corrupt giving of gifts.

Question: Why is this legislation a potential problem for promoters?

Answer: The long title of the legislation is given as 'An Act for the more effectual Prevention and Punishment of Bribery and Corruption of and by Members, Officers, or Servants of Corporations, Councils, Boards,

Commissions or other Public Bodies'. The relevance of Section 1 (which is paraphrased above), is that if an incentive scheme gives rise to corruption, the promoter will be open to prosecution for a criminal offence, as well as the recipient.

Question: How does the 1889 Act give us problems?

Answer: This Act, as its name suggests, is designed to protect the neutrality and impartiality of members of public authorities, officers of public authorities and public servants. This means that no bribes should be made to a public servant. In this regard it is important to note that 'public body' includes public authorities of all kinds, at both local and national level.

In addition, companies should be aware that the 1889 Act imposes a presumption that a gift or other consideration has been paid or given and received corruptly, unless the contrary is proved. And the penalties are much higher too in respect of public officials.

Question: What does 'bribery' mean in marketing terms?

Answer: 'Bribery' basically means offering an advantage to a public servant, in money or money's worth, which could influence the way he or she carries out his or her work, with the result that business favours are secured which would not otherwise be the case. The fact that it does not influence the public servant does not mean that an offence has not been committed; a charge of attempted bribery could be made. The important public policy consideration is that public servants should be above suspicion.

Therefore, no incentive scheme should be aimed at public servants. In any event, it is likely to be counter-productive to aim an incentive scheme at public servants because they will invariably have nothing to do with such approaches. Many will even refuse the offer of a free lunch.

Question: Does this apply to public servants in their private capacity?

Answer: No. The problem lies where the incentive is directed to them in their official capacity in a way that influences their judgment in relation to public issues.

Question: What about people other than public servants?

Answer: Apart from the 1889 Act there are the Prevention of Corruption Acts 1906–1916. Accordingly, there can be a problem if a gift or incentive to an individual employee causes, or is a potential cause, of a conflict of interests with his/her employer. Take a purchasing officer, for example. His/her duty is to purchase goods with only one consideration, the best interests of the company. If a promoter offers a purchasing officer a canteen of cutlery for purchasing from a particular supplier, then his/her personal interest and the company's interest may well conflict.

Question: Does the value of the incentive make any difference?

Answer: In practice it does, because if the value is not significant it is unlikely to be sufficient to encourage an employee to disregard his or her employer's interests. Accordingly, small gifts such as Christmas bottles of spirits are usually acceptable, but they should be carefully monitored, with an eye to avoiding any hint of a calculated effort to secure business favours.

Lessening the risk

Question: Is there any action I can take to lessen the risk of trouble?

Answer: Yes. First, it will help considerably if the employer is made aware of the incentive and gives consent. It is hard to see how an offence would arise if the employer is made aware of the scheme and does not object.

Secondly, the terms of the incentive should state that participation is dependent on the participants having the permission of the senior management.

Thirdly, it is important to make sure that the incentive is delivered to the company address and not a private residence.

Fourthly, where possible the incentive should be presented as a corporate benefit rather than an individual one.

Prosecutions

Question: Who can prosecute?

Answer: For a breach of s 1 of the 1889 Act a prosecution may only be instituted by or with the agreement of the Attorney General or the Solicitor General.

Question: What are the penalties?

Answer: On conviction or indictment at the crown court, a person is liable to imprisonment for a term not exceeding two years or to a fine or both. Where the offence relates to a contract or proposed contract with Her Majesty, a government department or a public body, the maximum sentence given is seven years imprisonment. In addition, the public official is liable to forfeit the gift, lose his or her public appointment and be banned from holding any public office for five years.

Question: Does the British Code of Advertising, Sales Promotion and Direct Marketing (the Code) have anything to say on this?

Answer: Yes. cl 38 of the Code covers trade incentives and it sets out a number of important rules. The important principle in the Code is that no trade incentive to employees should be such as to cause any conflict with the duty of employees to their employer, and that participating employees should normally secure the prior agreement of the employer or responsible manager. Trade incentives should not compromise the obligation of those employees giving advice to the public to give honest advice.

Question: Are there any controls which directly apply to purchasing officers?

Answer: Yes. Members of the Chartered Institute of Purchasing and Supply (CIPS) are required, as a condition of membership, to comply with the Institute's Professional Code of Ethics, which is designed to ensure that members never use their authority or office for personal gain and continually seek to uphold and enhance the purchasing and supply profession (the CIPS Professional Code of Ethics is set out as Appendix 5).

Tax

Question: Are there any tax implications?

Answer: An additional concern for promoters devising trade incentive schemes is the tax implications. Regard should be had, for example, to s 577 of the Income and Corporation Taxes Act 1988, which deals with business entertaining expenses.

The terms of the incentive should make clear to participants that there may be a tax liability, and that they should check their position.

Question: What about business gifts?

Answer: As we saw earlier, business gifts present the same potential problems as incentives. One must use common sense and consider certain factors, such as the position and remuneration level of the recipient, whether the recipient can provide business favours for the donor, and whether the gift has a business use.

Note: See also 'Tax and VAT' in Chapter 10.

MISCELLANEOUS LEGAL ISSUES

Age discrimination

Question: What relevance does age discrimination have to sales promotion and direct marketing?

Answer: The Government has made the Employment (Equality Age) Regulations 2006 which came into force in October 2006 and prohibit direct or indirect age discrimination. In particular, the rules cover employment benefits, employment rules, or any other practices that have the effect, without objective justification, of discriminating against people of a particular age. This has a particular relevance to incentive or motivation schemes.

Question: What about loyalty incentives?

Answer: Regulation 32 allows genuine schemes to continue; those that reward loyalty and experience and motivate staff. Their existence would not, therefore, constitute *unlawful* discrimination under the Regulations. However, any benefits offered under such schemes should not suggest an intention to discriminate on the basis of age.

Question: What action should I take to avoid contravening the regulations?

Answer: Companies should have a policy that relates to all anti-discrimination law. That policy should ensure that the range of benefits on offer do not unwittingly, and without objective justification, discriminate in favour of a particular age-group. In most cases, this will be a matter of commonsense. For example, a company whose loyalty benefits consisted wholly or largely of extreme sports activities might be seen to have discriminated indirectly against older employees. Help and advice can be obtained from the

Advisory Conciliation and Arbitration Service (ACAS). It can be contacted on 08456 003444.

Charity promotions

Question: Is there any special legislation affecting charity promotions?

Answer: Charity promotions are affected by the Charities Act 1992 and the Charitable Institutions (Fundraising) Regulations 1995. There are a number of implications for promoters, or commercial participators, as they are styled in the legislation. In any promotion which represents that charitable contributions are to be made, there has to be a clear statement indicating:

(a) the name or names of the institution or institutions concerned;

(b) if there is more than one institution concerned, the proportions in which the institutions are respectively to benefit; and

(c) (in general terms) the method by which it is to be determined:

   (i) what proportion of the consideration given for goods or services sold or supplied by him, or of any other proceeds of a promotional venture undertaken by him, is to be given to or applied for the benefit of the institution or institutions concerned, or

   (ii) what sums by way of donations by him in connection with the sale or supply of any such goods or services are to be so given or applied,

as the case may require.

The 1995 Regulations require a comprehensive written agreement between the charity and the promoter, covering all aspects of the promotion, including how the charity is to benefit and the obligations of the promoter.

Companies Act 2006

Question: Surely Companies legislation has nothing to tell us about the legality of sales promotion schemes?

Answer: Yes, it does. Although the Companies Act 2006 cannot be thought of as mainstream sales promotion legislation, it does have its implications. Section 82 of the Act provides power for the Secretary of State to make regulations requiring every company, inter alia, to include its name and specified information in specified documents and communications. Using these powers, the Secretary of State has made the Companies (Registrar, Languages and Trading Disclosures) Regulations 2006. The Regulations amend the Companies Act 1985 (the 1985 Act) by requiring all companies in the United Kingdom to include the following information on their websites and on electronic business letters and order forms:

* name of the UK registered company;

* place of registration;

* company registration number;

* registered office address.

This requirement extends to electronic business communications, the rules which have operated previously under the 1985 Act in respect of non-electronic communications.

Consumer credit

Question: How does consumer credit law control credit linked promotions?

Answer: The Consumer Credit Act 1974, as amended by the Consumer Credit Act 2006, and the regulations made thereunder include strict controls on advertising and other activities seeking business. The controls are as follows:

    (a) it is an offence to advertise goods or services on credit when it is not intended also to offer them for cash;

    (b) it is an offence to advertise credit facilities in a manner which is false or misleading in a material respect;

    (c) where an advertiser commits one of the offences given above, the publisher of the advertisement, any person who devised the advertisement and any person who procured the advertisement are also, subject to certain defences and exemptions, liable to prosecution;

    (d) it is an offence to canvass credit business off trade premises;

    (e) it is an offence to send a minor any document inviting him or her to borrow money, obtain goods or services on credit, or to apply for information or advice on borrowing money.

Question: Most credit linked promotions concern either a low or a no deposit credit deal or 0% interest finance. Are there any particular difficulties with this type of promotion?

Answer: Under the Consumer Credit (Advertisements) Regulations 2004, credit advertisements must give a comprehensive statement of the credit facilities on offer if the advertisements contains any of the following:

    (1) The frequency, number and amount of the repayments of the credit being offered;

    (2) A statement of any other payments and changes;

    (3) Total amount payable by the borrower.

There are also rules on the presentation of any required information and certain warnings which must be given, if relevant.

Very general references to credit do not normally trigger the requirement for further information and certain credit advertisements are exempt, for example an advertisement related solely to business credit and where credit is repayable in not more than four repayments over a period of twelve months.

Although these Regulations represent a simplification of the regulations which they replaced, it is still adviseable to seek professional advice on the form and content of credit advertisements.

Disability discrimination

Question: Do I need to worry about the Disability Discrimination Act 1995?

Answer: The Disability Discrimination Act 1995 (the 1995 Act), *as amended by the Disability Discrimination Act 2005,* makes it unlawful to discriminate in a number of ways against disabled persons. Discrimination is defined as the situation where, for a reason which relates to the disabled person's disability, he or she is treated less favourably than others. There is an exception where it can be shown that the treatment is justified by reference to a set of conditions set out in s 20(4) of the 1995 Act.

It is difficult to tell what effect disability discrimination legislation is going to have on the promotions industry. At the time of writing there have been no relevant cases and no directly relevant notes of guidance or codes of practice from the Commission for Equality and Human Rights—a body set up under the Equality Act 2006 to be responsible for the enforcement of all the legislation relating to discrimination and human rights. However, it is important that promoters have regard to the need not to discriminate unlawfully. It is also important that promoters contract with third party suppliers who do not discriminate unlawfully in the provision of goods or services to the public.

Informational requirements in direct response advertisements

Question: In a mail order advertisement or in a self-liquidating offer, people do not have the opportunity to inspect the goods before purchase. What effect does that have?

Answer: This means that legislation will apply that requires the provision of certain consumer information. For example, the Textile Products (Indications of Fibre Content) Regulations 1986, as amended by the Textile Products (Indications of Fibre Content)(Amendment and Consolidation of Schedules of Textile Names and Allowances) Regulations 2006 and the Textile Products (Determination of Composition) Regulations 2006, require details of fibre content to be given on labels attached to a product so that they can be seen before purchase. Obviously, if one is ordering goods on the strength of an advertisement or a promotional leaflet one cannot inspect the goods first. Accordingly, under regulation 6 one is required to give the information in the advertisement. The Regulation refers to advertisements 'intended for retail customers describing textile products with sufficient particularity to enable the products to be ordered by reference only to the description in the advertisement'.

A similar requirement exists under the Trade Descriptions (Sealskin Goods) (Information) Order 1980, under which information must be given with sealskin goods as to the fact that they are sealskin and the country in which the seals were killed. Article 5 applies this requirement to advertisements where there is no possibility of inspecting the goods first.

Finally, the same regime applies to direct response advertisements for nightwear. The Nightwear (Safety) Regulations 1985 require such advertisements to give information about the flammability of the product advertised.

Major sporting events

Question: We have been told that we can no longer offer tickets to major sporting events if we are not official sponsors or licensees. Is this true?

Answer: It has been common in the past for promoters to offer tickets to major sporting events without a formal relationship with the event. Tickets could be bought from a number of sources and then made the centre piece of a promotion. Except in relation to the Olympics (see below), the legal position has not changed but the practical environment has. This is as a result of increased litigiousness and the growth in official sponsorship and licensing. The position now is that, increasingly, the use of tickets from unauthorised sources will bring a challenge.

Question: Would any challenge be successful?

Answer: There is an absence of case law because the major events are generally unwilling to risk legal action in case they are unsuccessful. Far better from their point of view to exaggerate the legal rights available to event organisers and to bully as many promoters as possible who are running unauthorised promotions to pay some sort of licence fee. We do know, however, that in one case UEFA challenged a promotion involving a high street name and went so far as to go to court for an injunction. A central part of UEFA's argument was that the promoter was inducing a breach of contract. By approaching a person selling a ticket, the promoter was encouraging the seller to break the terms on which they had originally received the ticket, the point being that the official terms of ticket distribution forbade unauthorised use in promotions.

The case was never concluded because the promoter abandoned the promotion and settled the claim on terms which have been kept confidential.

Although the case never received a judicial ruling, it has demonstrated an increased willingness by bodies such as the UEFA to move beyond threats to actual court action. Therefore, the only safe advice to give the industry now is that no use should be made of tickets in a promotion unless they have come by lawfully and their use is consistent with the terms under which the tickets were originally issued.

Question: Are there any other legal issues involved?

Answer: Yes. Use of tickets which are unauthorised, or indeed any promotion which dovetails into a major sporting event, raises several legal issues.

First, there is the possibility of a challenge on the grounds of passing off. Basically, the argument would be that the promotion amounts to a misleading representation of a connection in the course of business between the promoter and the event—most usually on the basis that people would think that the promoter must be an official sponsor or licencee.

Secondly, there is the risk of an action for breach of copyright if some design work is shown, which attracts copyright protection such as the logo of the event.

Thirdly, there is also the possibility of an action for trade mark infringement which would probably be run in association with a claim for passing off. For, if the advertisement is misleading, the promoter would not be allowed to rely on the exception for what I would call 'honest identification use' in s 10(6) of the Trade Marks Act 1994.

Question: What about the Olympic Games?

Answer: The Olympic Games is in a somewhat special position because it is the subject of specific legislation. First, there is the Olympic Symbol etc (Protection) Act 1995. No use whatsoever can be made of the Olympic symbol and the Olympic motto unless one is an official licensee. There are also certain 'protected words' which are 'Olympiad', 'Olympiads', 'Olympian', 'Olympians', 'Olympic', 'Olympics', Paralympic, Paralympics, Paralympian, Paralympians, Paralympiad, Paralympiads and any word similar to the foregoing. However, so long as the words are used in a way that fairly represents a connection with the Olympic Games and are presented honestly, the use of any of these words will not infringe the Olympics Association right. This means that a hotel can describe itself as 'Handy for the Olympics'.

Secondly, we now have to contend with the London Olympic Games and Paralympic Games Act 2006 (the 2006 Act) which imposes a draconian regime on those who are not official sponsors or licensees.

Question: How does the 2006 Act affect promotions?

Answer: The new Act prohibits any attempt to make, in the course of business, any representation in a manner likely to create in the public mind an association with the London Olympics. A wide concept and one likely to be interpreted widely. To reinforce this, there are a number of words, the use of which will raise the possibility that such an association has been created. These words are in two groups, the first being 'games', 'Two Thousand and Twelve', '2012' and 'twenty twelve'. The second being 'gold', 'silver', 'bronze', 'London', 'medals', 'sponsor' and 'summer'.

Any combination of the expressions in the first group or any of the expressions in the second group when used with one or more expressions from the first group would give rise under the Act to the possibility of an infringement of the London Olympics Association Right. What this means is that it is going to become increasingly difficult for promoters to relate their promotions to the Olympic Games unless they are official sponsors or licensees.

Mock auctions

Question: Is there not something called the Mock Auctions Act? Does it have any relevance?

Answer: Yes, the Mock Auctions Act 1961 (the 1961 Act) makes it an offence to conduct a 'mock auction'.

This is defined as an auction at which one or more lots is sold to a person for less than the amount of the person's highest bid, or where part of the price is repaid or credited to him or her. Although it is not an enormously important legislation for the sales promotion industry it should be borne in mind, as it is easy to unwittingly contravene this Act.

For example, in one promotional idea, involving new cars, the public were to be invited to place bids for a new car and the highest bidder would obtain the car. However, the promoter proposed to add £1,000 to the bid of anyone who test drove the car. This meant that the car might go to a person who has part of his or her bid credited from the promoter.

Another problem the 1961 Act presents us with is that bidding cannot be restricted to those who have bought or agreed to buy one or more articles. For example, this would seem to catch promotions in which on the purchase of a product, say a pint of beer in a pub, one is given a token which can be used on an 'auction night'. It does not seem that this was the mischief which the Act sought to eliminate but it does, on the wording of the statute, pose a threat to such promotions. Accordingly, it may be wise to provide a free-entry route mechanism for people to acquire bidding tokens in such a promotion.

Origin marking

Question: Must imported promotion goods be marked with an indication of origin?

Answer: No. However, where an indication is likely to create the impression that the goods were produced or manufactured in a country other than that in which they were manufactured or produced, that statement should include a statement of the country where they were in fact manufactured or produced.

These requirements also apply to goods offered free of charge by way of promotions.

Package holidays

Question: If we organise a package holiday within a promotion, does this raise any special problems?

Answer: Yes. In certain circumstances, a holiday arranged as part of the promotion will be subject to the Foreign Package Holidays (Tour Operators and Travel Agents) Order 1998. Under the Order, it is unlawful for travel agents to discriminate in the price charged for a foreign package holiday or to impose an additional charge for travel insurance in respect of those who do not wish to buy insurance from that travel agent.

'Travel agent' is defined as 'a person who supplies or offers for supply a foreign package holiday put together by a tour operator'. It will be seen that this definition potentially affects a number of those organising overseas travel arrangements as part of a promotion. They should take note of the most important lesson of the Order which is that one should not make insurance obligatory from a particular supplier. It is, however, fine to require the travellers concerned to organise their own insurance.

Safety of promotional goods

Question: Are promotional goods subject to the law on consumer safety and if so, what are those laws?

Answer: Yes. The law on consumer safety is now contained in Pts I and II of the Consumer Protection Act 1987 (the 1987 Act), which has been extended by the General Product Safety Regulations 2005. That law relates to the 'supply' of dangerous goods, and thus goods offered free as incentives are subject to the law.

Part I of the 1987 Act imposes strict product liability. That means that any person who suffers damage to his or her person or to property can sue the producer of the product for unlimited damages without the need to prove the existence of a contract or negligence.

Part II of the Act, which has been amended by the General Product Safety Regulations 2005, requires that all consumer goods shall comply with the 'general safety requirement', ie they shall be as safe as may be reasonably expected. Any producer or distributor who supplies goods contrary to the general safety requirement is liable to prosecution.

Question: Who is liable if a person is injured by an incentive product?

Answer: The producer or distributor is liable. Where a retailer offers own-label products, the retailer is deemed to be 'holding himself out to be the producer' and is liable, unless the retailer makes it clear that the product is supplied to, or manufactured for, him or her.

Question: Who is liable in respect of the general safety requirement?

Answer: The position is quite different from Part I of the Act. Failure to comply with the general safety requirement is a criminal offence, and any producer or distributor who supplies consumer goods, or offers or agrees to supply such goods, or exposes or possesses such goods for supply which do not conform to the general safety requirement, is liable to prosecution.

Question: What is the general safety requirement?

Answer: Goods are deemed to fail to comply with the requirement if they are not reasonably safe, having regard to all the circumstances.

Tax and VAT

Question: What about tax implications?

Answer: There is a particular issue for incentive award schemes because the award is usually taxable. HM Revenue and Customs define an incentive award scheme as 'A way of rewarding employees and others with cash, goods or holidays rather than increases in pay.' They take a variety of forms and are usually linked to sales performance.

Question: How is tax liability arrived at?

Answer: In the case of cash awards, the amount chargeable to tax is the full amount of the award. For non-cash awards, the tax liability depends on the nature of the award. In the case of vouchers, the charge will be the cost to the provider of making the award.

Question: What if the employer or third party wishes to absorb the tax?

Answer: An arrangement can be made called a 'Taxed award scheme' in which it is agreed to pay the tax on a grossed up basis.

Question: How do I find out more?

Answer: Readers may be interested to know that guidance can be obtained from HM Revenue and Customs Incentive Valuation Unit, whose details are: Chapel Wharf Area, Trinity Bridge House, 2 Dearmans Place, Salford M3 5BH. Tel: 0161 261 3269.

Question: And VAT?

Answer: VAT is a complex subject in its own right, but it is worth mentioning the case of *Boots Company v The Commissioners of Customs and Excise* [1990]. The court decided that money-off coupons, obtained by consumers when they bought goods, are not a consideration when they are used to buy other goods. They are simply evidence of entitlement to a discount. Output VAT is therefore due only on the net amount which the consumer actually pays for the goods.

Tobacco advertising and promotion

Question: What is the position in respect of promotions for tobacco products?

Answer: The Tobacco Advertising and Promotion Act 2002 prohibits all advertising and promotion of tobacco products. There are very limited exceptions mainly applying to point of sale in relation to the premises of specialist tobacconists.

Using products in promotions

Question: Are there any risks in showing other company's products in a promotion?

Answer: Offering other company's products in promotions, particularly prize promotions, has been commonplace within the industry. However, as a result of an increased trend towards litigiousness, the use of other company's products within a promotion have to be seen as more risky today than before. The main risks are in relation to passing off and in relation to trade mark and copyright infringement.

Question: What are the copyright implications in showing another company's product?

Answer: Fortunately, s 51 of the Copyright, Designs and Patents Act 1988 tells us that it is not an infringement to copy an article if it has resulted from a design document or model recording or embodying the design. Since most products will start from a design document, it will not therefore normally be an infringement of copyright to feature such a product in a promotion. However, this does not apply to artistic works or to any surface decoration on the product. The product packaging will not be covered by s 51 nor will the logo of the company, which will also be a copyright work as well as possibly being a registered trade mark.

Question: Would it help if I took the brand name off the product?

Answer: In my view, one should only take the brand name off the product if in so doing the product looks like a generic item rather than one from a specific manufacturer; otherwise it may annoy the manufacturer to see that their brand name has been removed. In any event, s 10(6) of the Trade Marks Act 1994 allows what I would call honest identification use. As long as one is simply identifying the trade mark as that of the manufacturer and it is in the context of honest marketing communication, there will not be a trade mark infringement.

Question: What about the issue of passing off?

Answer: Passing off involves a misrepresentation which effectively piggy-backs off the commercial reputation of another trader. If a product is presented in such a way as to imply that the other company is a joint promoter or has in some way licenced or approved the use of the product in the promotion, there can be an argument about passing off. Promoters must therefore make sure that their copy does not suggest any such association with the company that manufactured the relevant goods.

Note: Changes to some of the subjects covered here will be occasioned by the implementation in the United Kingdom of the EU Unfair Commercial Practices Directive (UCPD).

The UCPD will introduce into U.K. law a general prohibition against unfair commercial practices. As a result, much existing legislation will be repealed and will be replaced by the coverage of the implementing regulations. These regulations will then form the basis of fair trading law in the United Kingdom.

At the time of writing, the implementing regulations have not been made and extensive discussions are taking place as to the balance between civil and criminal sanctions. The Regulations are likely to come into force some time in 2008.

CHAPTER 11

EUROPEAN ISSUES

Background

Question: What do people mean by the 'European Union'(EU)?

Answer: The Maastricht Treaty, or the Treaty on EU to give it its formal title, was signed on 7 February 1992, and came into operation on 1 November 1993. The Treaty created the EU and the concept of 'citizen of the Union'. However, contrary to popular view, the 'Union' is not a new name for the European Community (EC) or the European Economic Community (EEC).

In fact, the EU, when it was created, was like an umbrella under which the three original Treaties which make up the ECs continued. They were: (i) the European Coal and Steel Community Treaty (which expired in July 2002); (ii) the European Atomic Energy Community Treaty (Euratom); and, most importantly, (iii) the EEC Treaty, which has now been renamed the EC Treaty.

The EU also embraces provisions on co-operation in the fields of justice and home affairs, on a common foreign and security policy and special rules on social policy.

Question: Tell me more about the EC Treaty.

Answer: The EC is the successor to the EEC, which it replaced as a result of the Maastricht Treaty. The EC Treaty, which, as the EEC Treaty, was signed in Rome in 1957, is the bedrock of economic integration within Europe and it contains within it most of the important Treaty provisions that affect business and commerce within Europe. For example, within it are contained the rules on European competition law, and also the fundamental provisions on free movement of persons, goods and capital. And, as we shall see later on, the

EC Treaty has also been the basis for the development of the principles on freedom of movement of goods, which became so powerfully expressed in the famous *Cassis de Dijon* case.

Question: What are the main institutions of the EC?

Answer: The EC shares the same institutions with Euratom. These institutions are as follows:

(a)   The Council of the EU: The Council consists of a government minister from each Member State of the Community. The identity of that minister depends on the subject matter under discussion so that periodically there are meetings, for example, of agriculture ministers, transport ministers and consumer ministers. The chairmanship is taken in turns, giving each Member State six months in rotation.

(b)   The EC: The Commission is somewhat analogous to the UK civil service in that its functions are to develop proposals and implement agreed Community policies. Twenty-seven commissioners are appointed by the Member States—one for each country—and there is a staff of 24,000 civil servants. Unlike the Council, where national interests are paramount, the Commission is intended to operate in the interests of the Community as a whole.

Each commissioner has a five-year term, which may be renewed, and each assumes responsibility for a particular area, or 'portfolio', of Community business. The President of the Commission is chosen by EU Governments, subject to approval by the European Parliament.

(c)   The Court of Justice of the European Communities: The EU has its own legal order, arising from the treaties, and it takes precedence over the domestic law of each Member State. At the time of writing, the Court of Justice consists of 27 judges and 8 advocates-general, and is the final arbiter on matters of European law. Based in Luxembourg, the Court is frequently asked to give 'preliminary rulings' on points of European law referred to it by various national courts.

(d) The European Parliament: The role of the Parliament is largely consultative, although its influence has been growing since direct elections. Its 785 members serve for 5 years and they form their own political groupings. It is based in Luxembourg although it sometimes meets elsewhere, particularly in Brussels, where committee meetings are held. Plenary sessions are held in Strasbourg. Amongst other rights, it has the right to be consulted about Community legislation, to question members of the Commission and to reject the Community budget.

(e) The European Economic and Social Committee: The Committee, based in Brussels, is an advisory body designed to involve representatives of the various economic and social interest groups by giving them a vehicle for the expression of their views. Under the EC Treaty, the Council and the Commission must seek the views of the Committee on a wide range of issues. Membership of the Committee is in three groups: employers (group 1); trade unions (group 2); and various interests (group 3).

Commission involvement in marketing

Question: Why did the Commission get involved in the area of marketing?

Answer: There are two reasons why the EC is involved in the area of marketing.

First, there was the pressure to give the Community a human face in a Europe that appeared to be characterised by wine lakes and butter mountains. Accordingly, the EC launched its first Consumer Action Programme in 1974, and over the years a number of further consumer action programmes have followed. This has led to a number of measures in the consumer protection field which have a major impact on marketing, such as the Directives on Misleading Advertising, Distance Selling, and Product Liability. As a result of the Maastricht Treaty, consumer protection has been given a greatly enhanced role, and the Commission's Consumer Policy Service has been busy on a number of measures of concern to those in marketing; for example, in the area of consumer guarantees.

Secondly, the involvement of the Commission in the field of marketing is a natural consequence of the whole notion of an economic community, in which there is the progressive elimination of barriers. The push towards 1992 and the completion of the Internal Market involved consideration of barriers to cross-frontier trade. For this reason, the EC produced a Green Paper on Commercial Communications which examined comprehensively the restrictions that still exist on pan-European marketing in all the relevant marketing disciplines, and proposed a methodology for dealing with those restrictions.

Question: Tell me more about the Commercial Communications Green Paper.

Answer: In 1994, the EC began a massive review of the restrictions on marketing communications with the Single European Market. The Green Paper made its appearance in early 1996. It was a comprehensive study of all forms of advertising, direct marketing, sponsorship, sales promotions, and public relations promoting products and services within the EU.

There were five principal conclusions from the Green Paper:

(1) Cross-border commercial communication services in the Internal Market were a growing phenomenon.

(2) Differing national regulations created obstacles for companies wanting to offer such services across national borders and also created problems for consumers seeking redress against unlawful cross-border commercial communication services.

(3) Some of these divergences between the regulatory frameworks of Member States could give rise to barriers as more commercial communication services circulate across borders.

(4) The risk of such regulatory differences giving rise to barriers may be accentuated with the advent of the new services developed in the Information Society.

(5) The availability of information about regulatory measures and market developments was becoming increasingly important at the national and community level.

The Green Paper made three important proposals. The first consisted of establishing a proportionality assessment procedure to gauge compatibility with European law. The second consisted of establishing a committee of representatives from the Member States that would review such problems. The third was a central contact point which would receive complaints and provide information on all Community law in this field.

Question: Will we ever have a completed Internal Market in respect of promotional marketing?

Answer: In October 2001, the European Commission proposed a Council and European Parliament Regulation to remove restrictions on sales promotions within the Internal Market that were identified by the Commission in their Green Paper on Commercial Communications. Several drafts were produced but in the end the Draft Sales Promotion Regulation was shelved. It remains to be seen how long it takes for the issue to be raised again.

European legislation

Question: I understand about UK legislation, but I am confused about the legislation that comes from Brussels and the form it takes.

Answer: There are two main forms of legislation emanating from the EU: Directives and Regulations.

(a)   EC Directives: Article 249 of the consolidated EC Treaty says: 'A Directive shall be binding as to the result to be achieved, upon each Member State to which it is addressed, but shall leave to the national authorities the choice of form and methods.' The Member States are given a period, usually two years, in which to give effect to the Directive. The European Court has considerably extended the importance of directives so that in certain circumstances individuals can claim damages for their non-implementation.

(b)   EC Regulations: Article 249 says: 'A Regulation shall have general application. It shall be binding in its entirety and is directly applicable in all Member States.' Unlike a Directive, a Regulation lays down immediate legal obligations throughout the Community. Regulations are usually made where it is necessary to have common European rules, usually on technical issues.

Cassis de Dijon

Question: Much has been made over the years of the *Cassis de Dijon* case in the context of European marketing. Why?

Answer: Article 29 of the EC Treaty is the legal bedrock of free circulation of goods within the Community. It forbids the Member States to institute quantitative restrictions on imports and any measures having equivalent effect. A long line of cases on this article have arisen in the Court of Justice over the years—the most famous of which is *Cassis de Dijon* [1979].

The *Cassis* case involved the famous French blackcurrant liqueur. As produced in France, it contained 15–20 per cent alcohol by volume. Problems arose in relation to its importation into Germany, because German law required such a product to have at least 32 per cent alcohol. It could be imported into Germany, but it was not possible to market it as 'Creme de Cassis'.

The European Court held that such indirect discrimination fell foul of art 29 (as it now is) and, since the German rule could not be justified on other grounds, it was contrary to the Treaty. Accordingly, the case opened up the markets of Europe to cross-frontier trade, even where the national marketing restrictions applied to imports and domestic industry alike.

Although the case law of the European Court on art 29 has varied over the years—sometimes in a seemingly contradictory way—the present position appears to be that an obstacle to the free movement of goods is unlawful under European law unless the restrictions apply equally to domestic as well as imported goods. Such restrictions must also be necessary to genuinely satisfy requirements relating to such matters as consumer protection and must be proportionate to the intended purpose. So, for example, in a case in 1990, a Belgian supermarket was able to overturn a conviction under Luxembourg law relating to the distribution of leaflets which offered a reduced price offer and gave the original higher prices.

Different national rules

Question: Is it correct to say that national rules in the United Kingdom on sales promotion and direct marketing are the most liberal in Europe?

Answer: Yes, although Ireland's rules are very similar.

Germany has the most restrictive rules although some liberalisation has taken place, particularly as a result of the new Competition Act. Traditionally, premiums have only been allowed if a reasonable price is charged, or the premium is of insignificant value, or it can be regarded as a product accessory.

Other EU countries have serious restrictions on promotions. For example, France has limits on the value of premiums—7 per cent of the selling price of the purchased article. Free draws and instant win mechanics are sometimes not allowed in Germany, Austria and Switzerland. Depending on the value, free gifts can also be a problem in those countries, and in France a nominal price has to be charged for the 'free gift' unless certain limited exceptions apply.

Generally speaking, the more northerly countries are more restrictive than the southern ones. Those countries like Germany, which heavily restrict sales promotion, do so because they believe that promotional techniques have the effect of deflecting the consumer's attention from rational purchasing decisions based on an objective analysis of a product's characteristics.

Question: I understand Ireland is a problem on prize promotions?

Answer: Yes. The Irish legislation is the Gaming and Lotteries Act 1956—a very similar piece of legislation to the UK's Lotteries and Amusements Act 1976. However, in relation to instant wins and similar schemes, the Irish Supreme Court has concluded that most, if not all, such schemes are illegal lotteries in Ireland.

In the case of *Flynn and Denieffe v Independent Newspapers Plc* in 1992, the Court concluded that as the overwhelming majority of people had bought a newspaper in order to participate, it did not matter that they could have entered without purchase. Blayney J. concluded:

> 'The fact that persons who had not purchased a newspaper could take part in no way prevented the scheme being a lottery vis-à-vis those whose participation resulted from purchasing a newspaper.'

This decision creates a substantial difference between what is regarded as acceptable in the United Kingdom and what is acceptable in the Irish Republic. It has made prize promotions aimed at both the United Kingdom and the Irish Republic problematic and professional advice is needed.

Question: What about other European countries?

Answer: As we have seen, the national rules on sales promotion vary considerably across the EU, and in order to run a pan-European promotion at present one needs advice on the position in each individual country.

European self-regulation

Question: Does self-regulation operate across Europe?

Answer: Self-regulation in Europe operates principally on the basis of national systems and national codes. There is a great deal of similarity between these codes, not least because they owe much of their inspiration to the Codes of Marketing Practice produced by the International Chamber of Commerce (ICC). These Codes, as of 2006, have been consolidated into one ICC Code entitled 'Advertising and marketing communication practice'.

However, a measure of co-ordination of national self-regulation is achieved through the the European Advertising Standards Alliance (EASA).

EASA brings together the advertising self-regulatory organisations from 23 European countries and from 5 non-European countries. Though EASA has developed a system that makes it possible for consumers to complain about a cross-border advertisement or sales promotion simply by writing to the complainant's own national advertising self–regulatory body, such as the Advertising Standards Authority (ASA) in the United Kingdom.

If the complaint turns out to be a cross-border complaint, it is passed to the relevant self-regulatory body in the country of origin of the medium in which the advertisement appeared. It is then checked for compliance with the rules set out in that country's code of practice on marketing communications.

CHAPTER 12

SALES PROMOTION AND DIRECT MARKETING ADMINISTRATION CHECKLIST

There is an old saying that a chain is as strong as its weakest link. Nowhere is this more true than in the world of sales promotion. A lot of links in the chain have to hang together effectively for a promotion to be a success. So, many of the sales promotion schemes that feature in the case reports of the Advertising Standards Authority (ASA) are not the result of a failure by the promoter and its agency to appreciate the law and the codes; rather they are the result of various failures of administration.

Another thought to concentrate the mind is that the cost of a failure of administration can be truly colossal. Potentially, a promotion that goes wrong can be much more expensive to a company than an advertising campaign which goes wrong. As someone put it to me: 'The ending of a promotion can require just as much thought as the beginning of one.'

This book is not the place for a detailed consideration of such issues, but I have taken the opportunity to set out a checklist of some of the major issues affecting the administration of a promotion. From experience, I know how crucial such issues are to a promotion's success.

(a) *Taking sales promotion and direct marketing seriously:* Within marketing departments of major companies, there has been a tendency to regard sales promotion and other 'below the line' activities as the Cinderella of the marketing mix. Some years ago, an advertising agency executive said to me that, whereas sales promotion was a mechanical operation, advertising was a cerebral activity. This snobbish view about the role of sales promotion means that decisions relating to sales promotion have all too often not been taken at a senior enough level within the company, and this in itself can lead to problems of administration.

Fortunately, the growth of sales promotion as a marketing discipline has necessitated a re-evaluation of its importance by other marketing disciplines, and by those in the marketing departments of major companies. This is crucial, as one of the prime considerations in sales promotion schemes being effective is that companies take sales promotion as a marketing discipline as seriously as they do advertising and other marketing disciplines.

(b) *Taking administration seriously:* Quite rightly, many in the industry see creativity as the key to a successful promotion. And creativity is important in making an impact in a highly competitive marketplace. But a successful promotion also needs to be professionally administered in all its stages if consumers are not to be disadvantaged. It may not be glamorous and it may not win industry awards, but its importance cannot be underestimated.

(c) *Outside suppliers:* Inevitably, promoters frequently need to use outside suppliers in order to fulfil the needs of a promotion, whether it is a sourcing company, a travel company or a handling house. It is crucial that the promoter makes sure that the outside companies that they use to fulfil the promotion are up to the job. Many promoters take little interest in the standing and position of outside suppliers, or with supervising their work, with the result that the reputation of the promoter itself suffers.

Promoters must institute appropriate checks into the standing and effectiveness of the outside companies that they use and, in appropriate cases, they should use only those companies that are members of an association which has a recognised code of practice. For example, in the case of handling houses it is important that promoters use only those companies that are willing to adhere to the ISP's 'Guidelines for briefing fulfilment houses' (reproduced in Appendix 4, below).

(d) *Contracts:* In order to run a successful promotion, a great many relationships need to function effectively and this is where careful drafting of contracts becomes important. Apart from the contract between agency and promoter, there will be many others with those who are responsible for fulfilling the promotion, such as printers, sourcing companies and handling houses. Particularly important are the fundamental questions of who does what and when. Issues of quality are fundamental, particularly in contracts with sourcing companies.

There are, of course, many other issues to consider but the fundamental point is that the good administration of a promotion requires clear and comprehensive contracts.

(e) *Effective communication:* Time and time again, a promotion fails and falls foul of the British Code of Advertising, Sales Promotion and Direct Marketing (CAP Code) because of inadequate briefing. It is no good for the marketing department to be clear in their own mind what needs to happen for a promotion to be legally sound and in compliance with the Code, if the people who need to operate the promotion down the line are not properly briefed. Effective communication and briefing of all those involved in a promotion is therefore crucial.

(f) *Careful estimations:* A successful promotion requires a careful estimate of likely consumer demand from the promotion, and proper arrangements to meet that demand. This is by far one of the most important administrative aspects of running a promotion. Indeed, the CAP Code requires promoters to make a reasonable pre-estimate of likely demand. This is not just a Code requirement; it is also a commercial necessity.

(g) *Realistic budgets:* Akin to making a careful estimate of likely demand is to make sure the budget for the promotion is adequate to the likely demand.

(h) *Realistic timetables:* So often, unrealistic timetables are included within a promotion. This is particularly true of competitions that involve a lengthy judging process. A timetable for judging and awarding of prizes needs to be instituted, and not infrequently this cannot be met and, therefore, there is a problem of slippage of dates. It is crucial that realistic dates are set for a promotion, ie dates that the promoter knows can be complied with, and which make allowances for absences and the natural delaying factors which arise in everyday life.

(i) *Check and double-check:* So many promoters have come adrift over the years because assumptions have been made, particularly assumptions that other people have done what is required of them.

It is important for promoters to check and re-check every aspect of a promotion to make sure that everything that should happen, does happen, and that everybody who has a role to play meets his or her obligations. Some of the worst catastrophes in sales promotion have arisen because assumptions have been made, particularly assumptions that people can be relied on, when they cannot.

(j) *Complaints:* Dealing with complaints in respect of the promotion is an important challenge for promoters. One should always deal positively with complaints, whether they are justified or unjustified; there is nothing worse than a weak and vacillating response.

If the complaint is justified, then by far the best way to defuse the issue is to apologise and make an appropriate gesture of amends. Nothing keeps an issue alive more effectively than for a company to prevaricate and make excuses when it is patently obvious to an independent observer that some mistake has been made and the company is trying to cover up. At the end of the day, the company gains more credit from an open acknowledgement and apology.

If, on the other hand, the complaint is groundless, then it is important that a firm and resolute response is given, and important that no token is given which could be interpreted as an acknowledgement of weakness on the part of the promoter. If the promoter's position is sound, then the promoter must stand firm.

(k) *Keep records:* There are a number of competition enthusiasts, known in the trade as 'compers'. Some are prepared to challenge the adjudication on competitions—in some cases several years after the competition has been run. In addition, there are growing numbers of people prepared to challenge the way in which promotions are organised and administered.

In order to deal properly with these challenges, a promoter must keep proper records and for a reasonable period of time. It is difficult to say what that period should be, but in my view in the case of prize competitions and games of chance I would recommend two years and I would recommend at least one year from the end of the promotion in the case of other promotional mechanics.

Some concern has been expressed as to whether keeping promotion records for any length of time conflicts with Data Protection Principle 5: 'Personal data processed for any purpose or purposes shall not be kept longer than is necessary for that purpose or purposes.' We have no guidance on this point from the Information Commissioner's office, nor are there are relevant cases to which we can refer. It is therefore a commonsense judgement that we need to apply. This, in my view, means keeping records for as long as is reasonably necessary to see whether any challenge is made. If any challenge is made, the records should then be kept for a much longer period.

(l) *Checklist:* It is important for those in the sales promotion industry to develop their own checklists in order to ensure a systematic approach to the creation, planning and administration of each promotion. The issues we have discussed here should provide a basis for such a checklist.

(m) *'The secretary test':* Those who give professional advice about promotions know only too well that the most valuable service that can be rendered in respect of a promotion is often the provision of an independent view. We often cannot see clearly something that we are closely involved in, and we need an independent third party to look at what we are doing.

Accordingly, there is much to be said for getting such an independent person to read through the material for a promotion, because he or she can look at a promotion very much through the eyes of an ordinary consumer, without the inside knowledge and experience of those who put the promotion together. So often agencies and promoters have persuaded themselves that a particular piece of wording is clear. Yet the moment that material is seen by a third party it is patently obvious that it is far from clear, and is actually highly ambiguous, to say the least.

That independent third party can be anybody, but I call this test 'the secretary test' because secretaries are often blessed with a considerable degree of common sense and this makes them peculiarly well suited to giving a view about the wording and presentation of a promotion.

APPENDICES

THE BRITISH CODE OF ADVERTISING, SALES PROMOTION AND DIRECT MARKETING

Published by, and reproduced here with the permission of, the Committee of Advertising Practice (CAP), Mid City Place, 71 High Holborn, London, WC1V 6QT. Tel: 020 7492 2222. Fax: 020 7242 3696. Internet: http://www.cap.org.uk

In the United Kingdom, the British Code of Advertising, Sales Promotion and Direct Marketing (the Code) is the rule book for non-broadcast advertisements, sales promotions and direct marketing communications (marketing communications). The Code is primarily concerned with the content of marketing communications and not with terms of business or products themselves.

Some rules, however, go beyond content, for example, those that cover the administration of sales promotions, the suitability of promotional items, the delivery of products ordered through an advertisement and the use of personal information in direct marketing. Editorial content is specifically excluded from the Code, although it might be a factor in determining the context in which marketing communications are judged.

The Committee of Advertising Practice (CAP) is the self-regulatory body that creates, revises and enforces the Code. CAP's members include organisations that represent the advertising, sales promotion, direct marketing and media businesses. Through their membership of CAP member organisations, or through contractual agreements with media publishers and carriers, those businesses agree to comply with the Code so that marketing communications are legal, decent, honest and truthful and consumer confidence is maintained.

Some CAP member organisations, for example, the Direct Marketing Association (DMA) and the Proprietary Association of Great Britain, also require their members to observe their own codes of practice. Those codes may cover some practices that are not covered in this Code.

The Code supplements the law, fills gaps where the law does not reach and often provides an easier way of resolving disputes than by civil litigation or criminal prosecution. In many cases, self-regulation ensures that legislation is not necessary. Although advertisers, promoters and direct marketers (marketers), agencies and media may still wish to consult lawyers, compliance with the Code should go a long way to ensuring compliance with the law in areas covered by both the Code and the law.

By creating and following self-imposed rules, the marketing community produces marketing communications that are welcomed and trusted. By practising self-regulation, it ensures the integrity of advertising, promotions and direct marketing.

The value of self-regulation as an alternative to statutory control is recognised in EC Directives, including those on misleading and comparative advertising (Directives 84/450 and 97/55 EC), and self-regulation is accepted by the Department of Trade and Industry and the Office of Fair Trading (OFT) as a first line of control in protecting consumers.

The Advertising Standards Authority (ASA) is the independent body that endorses and administers the Code, ensuring that the self-regulatory system works in the public interest. The ASA's activities include investigating and adjudicating on complaints and conducting research.

A leaflet describing the ASA's complaints procedure is available on request and full information is available on www.asa.org.uk.

The vast majority of advertisers, promoters and direct marketers comply with the Code. Those that do not may be subject to sanctions. Adverse publicity may result from the rulings published by the ASA weekly on its website. The media, contractors and service providers may withhold their services or deny access to space. Trading privileges (including direct mail discounts) and recognition may be revoked, withdrawn or temporarily withheld. Pre-vetting may be imposed and, in some cases, non-complying parties can be referred to the OFT for action, where appropriate, under the Control of Misleading Advertisements Regulations.

The system is structured so that it does not operate in an unfair or anti-competitive manner or restrict free speech unjustifiably. ASA decisions are subject to independent review, including in exceptional cases by the Administrative Division of the High Court.

The full text of the Code is available on www.cap.org.uk.

Mid City Place 71 High Holborn London WC1V 6QT

CAP: t 020 7492 2200 f 020 7404 3404 e enquiries@cap.org.uk www.cap.org.uk

ASA: t 020 7492 2222 f 020 7242 3696 e enquiries@asa.org.uk www.asa.org.uk

Contents

Members of the CAP

Advertising Association

Broadcast Advertising Clearance Centre

Cinema Advertising Association

Direct Marketing Association

Direct Selling Association

Incorporated Society of British Advertisers

Institute of Practitioners in Advertising

Institute of Sales Promotion

Interactive Advertising Bureau

Mail Order Traders Association

Newspaper Publishers Association

Newspaper Society

Outdoor Advertising Association

Periodical Publishers Association

Proprietary Association of Great Britain

Radio Advertising Clearance Centre

Royal Mail

Scottish Daily Newspaper Society

Scottish Newspaper Publishers Association

Introduction

This 11th edition of the Code comes into force on 4 March 2003. It replaces all previous editions.

1.1   The Code applies to:

a   advertisements in newspapers, magazines, brochures, leaflets, circulars, mailings, e-mails, text transmissions, fax transmissions, catalogues, follow-up literature and other electronic and printed material

b   posters and other promotional media in public places, including moving images

c   cinema and video commercials

d   advertisements in non-broadcast electronic media, including online advertisements in paid-for space (eg, banner and pop-up advertisements)

e   viewdata services

f   marketing databases containing consumers' personal information

g   sales promotions

h   advertisement promotions

1.2   The Code does not apply to:

a   broadcast commercials. (The Broadcast Committee of Advertising Practice [BCAP] Advertising Standards Codes set out the rules that govern broadcast advertisements on any television channel and radio station licensed by Ofcom)

b   the contents of premium rate services, which are the responsibility of the Independent Committee for the Supervision of Standards of Telephone Information Services (ICSTIS); marketing communications that promote these services are subject to ICSTIS regulation and to the Code

c   marketing communications in foreign media. Direct marketing that originates outside the United Kingdom but is targeted at UK consumers will be subject to the jurisdiction of the relevant authority in the country where it originates so long as that authority operates a suitable cross-border complaint system. If it does not, the ASA will take what action it can. All members of the European Union, and many non-European countries, have self-regulatory organisations (SROs) that are members of the European Advertising Standards Alliance (EASA). EASA co-ordinates the cross-border complaints system for its members (which include the ASA).

d   health-related claims in marketing communications addressed only to the medical, dental, veterinary and allied professions

e   classified private advertisements, including those appearing online

f   statutory, public, police and other official notices/information, as opposed to marketing communications, produced by public authorities and the like

g   works of art exhibited in public or private

h   private correspondence, including correspondence between companies and their customers about existing relationships or past purchases

i   live oral communications, including telephone calls

j   press releases and other public relations material, so long as they do not fall under 1.1 above

k   editorial content, for example, of the media and of books

l   regular competitions such as crosswords

m   flyposting (most of which is illegal)

n   packages, wrappers, labels, tickets, timetables and price lists unless they advertise another product, a sales promotion or are visible in a marketing communication

o   point of sale displays, except those covered by the sales promotion rules and the rolling paper and filter rules

p   election advertisements as defined in cl 12.1

q   website content, except sales promotions and advertisements in paid-for space

r   sponsorship; marketing communications that refer to sponsorship are covered by the Code

s   customer charters and codes of practice.

1.3   These definitions apply to the Code:

a   a *product* encompasses goods, services, ideas, causes, opportunities, prizes or gifts

b   a *consumer* is anyone who is likely to see a given marketing communication, whether in the course of business or not

c   the *United Kingdom* rules cover the Isle of Man and the Channel Islands

d   a *claim* can be implied or direct, written, spoken or visual

e   the Code is divided into numbered *clauses*

f   a *marketing communication* includes all forms of communication listed in 1.1

g   a *marketer* includes an advertiser, promoter or direct marketer

h   a *supplier* is anyone who supplies products that are sold by distance selling marketing communications (and may also be the marketer)

i   a *child* is anyone under 16.

j   a *corporate subscriber* includes corporate bodies such as limited companies in the United Kingdom, limited liability partnerships in England, Wales and N. Ireland or any partnerships in Scotland. It also includes schools, hospitals, Government departments or agencies and other public bodies. It does not include sole traders or non-limited liability partnerships in England, Wales and N. Ireland. See cl 43.4

1.4   These criteria apply to the Code:

a   the ASA Council's interpretation of the Code is final

b conformity with the Code is assessed according to the marketing communication's probable impact when taken as a whole and in context. This will depend on the medium in which the marketing communication appeared, the audience and its likely response, the nature of the product and any additional material distributed to consumers

c the Code is indivisible; marketers must conform with all appropriate rules

d the Code does not have the force of law and its interpretation will reflect its flexibility. The Code operates alongside the law; the Courts may also make rulings on matters covered by the Code

e an indication of the statutory rules governing marketing is given on www.cap.org.uk; professional advice should be taken if there is any doubt about their application

f no spoken or written communications with the ASA or CAP should be understood as containing legal advice

g the Code is primarily concerned with the content of advertisements, promotions and direct marketing communications and not with terms of business or products themselves. Some rules, however, go beyond the content, for example, those that cover the administration of sales promotions, the suitability of promotional items, the delivery of products ordered through an advertisement and the use of personal information in direct marketing. Editorial content is specifically excluded from the remit of the Code (see 1.2k), although it might be a factor in determining the context in which marketing communications are judged (see 1.4b)

h the rules make due allowance for public sensitivities but will not be used by the ASA to diminish freedom of speech unjustifiably

i the ASA does not arbitrate between conflicting ideologies.

General rules

Principles

2.1 All marketing communications should be legal, decent, honest and truthful.

2.2   All marketing communications should be prepared with a sense of responsibility to consumers and to society.

2.3   All marketing communications should respect the principles of fair competition generally accepted in business.

2.4   No marketing communication should bring advertising into disrepute.

2.5   Marketing communications must conform with the Code. Primary responsibility for observing the Code falls on marketers. Others involved in preparing and publishing marketing communications such as agencies, publishers and other service suppliers also accept an obligation to abide by the Code.

2.6   Any unreasonable delay in responding to the ASA's enquiries may be considered a breach of the Code.

2.7   The ASA and CAP will on request treat in confidence any genuinely private or secret material supplied unless the Courts or officials acting within their statutory powers compel its disclosure.

2.8   The Code is applied in the spirit as well as in the letter.

Substantiation

3.1   Before distributing or submitting a marketing communication for publication, marketers must hold documentary evidence to prove all claims, whether direct or implied, that are capable of objective substantiation.

Relevant evidence should be sent without delay if requested by the ASA or CAP. The adequacy of evidence will be judged on whether it supports both the detailed claims and the overall impression created by the marketing communication. The full name and geographical business address of marketers should be provided without delay if requested by the ASA or CAP.

3.2   If there is a significant division of informed opinion about any claims made in a marketing communication they should not be portrayed as generally agreed.

3.3   Claims for the content of non-fiction books, tapes, videos and the like that have not been independently substantiated should not

exaggerate the value, accuracy, scientific validity or practical useful-
ness of the product.

3.4 Obvious untruths or exaggerations that are unlikely to mislead
and incidental minor errors and unorthodox spellings are all allowed
provided they do not affect the accuracy or perception of the marketing
communication in any material way. ·

Legality

4.1 Marketers have primary responsibility for ensuring that their marketing communications are legal. Marketing communications should
comply with the law and should not incite anyone to break it.

Decency (ie, avoiding serious or widespread offence)

5.1 Marketing communications should contain nothing that is likely
to cause serious or widespread offence. Particular care should be taken
to avoid causing offence on the grounds of race, religion, sex, sexual
orientation or disability.

Compliance with the Code will be judged on the context, medium,
audience, product and prevailing standards of decency.

5.2 Marketing communications may be distasteful without necessarily conflicting with 5.1 above. Marketers are urged to consider public
sensitivities before using potentially offensive material.

5.3 The fact that a particular product is offensive to some people
is not sufficient grounds for objecting to a marketing communication
for it.

Honesty

6.1 Marketers should not exploit the credulity, lack of knowledge or
inexperience of consumers.

Truthfulness

7.1 No marketing communication should mislead, or be likely
to mislead, by inaccuracy, ambiguity, exaggeration, omission or
otherwise.

Matters of opinion

8.1   Marketers may give a view about any matter, including the qualities or desirability of their products, provided it is clear that they are expressing their own opinion rather than stating a fact. Assertions that go beyond subjective opinions are subject to 3.1 above (also see 12.1 below).

Fear and distress

9.1   No marketing communication should cause fear or distress without good reason. Marketers should not use shocking claims or images merely to attract attention.

9.2   Marketers may use an appeal to fear to encourage prudent behaviour or to discourage dangerous or ill-advised actions; the fear likely to be aroused should not be disproportionate to the risk.

Safety

10.1   Marketing communications should not condone or encourage unsafe practices. Particular care should be taken with marketing communications addressed to or depicting children (see s 47).

10.2   Consumers should not be encouraged to drink and drive. Marketing communications should, where appropriate, include a prominent warning on the dangers of drinking and driving and should not suggest that the effects of drinking alcohol can be masked.

Violence and anti-social behaviour

11.1   Marketing communications should contain nothing that condones or is likely to provoke violence or anti-social behaviour.

Political advertising

12.1   Any advertisement or direct marketing communication, whenever published or distributed, whose principal function is to influence voters in local, regional, national or international elections or referendums is exempt from the Code.

12.2   There is a formal distinction between Government policy and that of political parties. Marketing communications (see cll 1.1 and

1.2) by central or local government, as distinct from those concerning party policy, are subject to the Code.

Protection of privacy

13.1 Marketers should not unfairly portray or refer to people in an adverse or offensive way. Marketers are urged to obtain written permission before:

a   referring to or portraying members of the public or their identifiable possessions; the use of crowd scenes or general public locations may be acceptable without permission

b   referring to people with a public profile; references that accurately reflect the contents of books, articles or films may be acceptable without permission

c   implying any personal approval of the advertised product; marketers should recognise that those who do not wish to be associated with the product may have a legal claim.

13.2   Prior permission may not be needed when the marketing communication contains nothing that is inconsistent with the position or views of the person featured.

13.3   References to anyone who is deceased should be handled with particular care to avoid causing offence or distress.

13.4   Members of the Royal Family should not normally be shown or mentioned in marketing communications without their prior permission. Incidental references unconnected with the advertised product, or references to material such as books, articles or films about members of the Royal Family, may be acceptable.

13.5   The Royal Arms and Emblems should be used only with the prior permission of the Lord Chamberlain's office. References to Royal Warrants should be checked with the Royal Warrant Holders' Association.

Testimonials and endorsements

14.1   Marketers should hold signed and dated proof, including a contact address, for any testimonial they use. Unless they are genuine opinions taken from a published source, testimonials should be used only with the written permission of those giving them.

14.2   Testimonials should relate to the product being advertised.

14.3   Testimonials alone do not constitute substantiation and the opinions expressed in them must be supported, where necessary, with independent evidence of their accuracy. Any claims based on a testimonial must conform with the Code.

14.4   Fictitious testimonials should not be presented as though they are genuine.

14.5   Unless they are genuine statements taken from a published source, references to tests, trials, professional endorsements, research facilities and professional journals should be used only with the permission of those concerned.

14.6   Marketers should not refer in marketing communications to advice received from CAP or imply any endorsement by the ASA or CAP.

Prices

(see CAP Help Notes on Lowest Price Claims and Price Promises and on Retailers' Price Comparisons)

15.1   Any stated price should be clear and should relate to the product advertised. Marketers should ensure that prices match the products illustrated (see 48.7).

15.2   Prices quoted in marketing communications addressed to the public should include VAT and other non-optional taxes and duties imposed on all buyers. In some circumstances, for example, where marketing communications are likely to be read mainly by businesses able to recover VAT, prices may be quoted exclusive of VAT or other taxes and duties, provided prominence is given to the amount or rate of any additional costs.

15.3   If the price of one product is dependent on the purchase of another, the extent of any commitment by consumers must be made clear.

15.4   Price claims such as 'up to' and 'from' should not exaggerate the availability of benefits likely to be obtained by consumers.

15.5 A recommended retail price (RRP), or similar, used as a basis of comparison should be genuine; it should not differ significantly from the price at which the product is generally sold.

Availability of products

16.1 Marketers must make it clear if stocks are limited. Products must not be advertised unless marketers can demonstrate that they have reasonable grounds for believing that they can satisfy demand. If a product becomes unavailable, marketers will be required to show evidence of stock monitoring, communications with outlets and swift withdrawal of marketing communications whenever possible.

16.2 Products which cannot be supplied should not normally be advertised as a way of assessing potential demand unless it is clear that this is the purpose of the marketing communication.

16.3 Marketers must not use the technique of switch selling, where their sales staff criticise the advertised product or suggest that it is not available and recommend the purchase of a more expensive alternative. They should not place obstacles in the way of purchasing the product or delivering it promptly.

Guarantees

(see CAP Help Note on Lowest Price Claims and Price Promises)

17.1 Guarantees may be legally binding on those offering them. The word 'guarantee' should not be used in a way that could cause confusion about consumers' legal rights. Substantial limitations on the guarantee should be spelled out in the marketing communication. Before commitment, consumers should be able to obtain the full terms of the guarantee from marketers.

17.2 Marketers should inform consumers about the nature and extent of any additional rights provided by the guarantee, over and above those given to them by law, and should make clear how to obtain redress.

17.3 Marketers should provide a cash refund, postal order or personal cheque promptly to those claiming redress under a money-back guarantee.

Comparisons with identified competitors and/or their products

18.1 Comparative claims are permitted in the interests of vigorous competition and public information. They should neither mislead nor be likely to mislead.

18.2 They should compare products meeting the same needs or intended for the same purpose.

18.3 They should objectively compare one or more material, relevant, verifiable and representative features of those products, which may include price.

18.4 They should not create confusion between marketers and competitors or between marketers' products, trade marks, trade names or other distinguishing marks and those of competitors.

18.5 Certain EU agricultural products and foods are, because of their unique geographical area and method of production, given special protection by being registered as having a 'designation of origin'. Products with a designation of origin should be compared only with other products with the same designation.

Other comparisons

19.1 Other comparisons, for example, those with marketers' own products, those with products of others who are not competitors or those that do not identify competitors or their products explicitly or by implication, should be clear and fair. They should neither mislead nor be likely to mislead. The elements of comparisons should not be selected in a way that gives the marketers an artificial advantage.

Denigration and unfair advantage

20.1 Although comparative claims are permitted, marketing communications that include comparisons with identifiable competitors and/or their products should not discredit or denigrate the products, trade marks, trade names, other distinguishing marks, activities or circumstances of competitors. Other marketing communications should not unfairly attack or discredit businesses or their products.

20.2   Marketers should not take unfair advantage of the reputation of trade marks, trade names or other distinguishing marks of organisations or of the designation of origin of competing products.

Imitation

21.1   No marketing communication should so closely resemble any other that it misleads, is likely to mislead or causes confusion.

21.2   Marketers making comparisons with identifiable competitors and/or their products should not present products as imitations or replicas of products bearing a protected trade mark or trade name.

Recognising marketing communications and identifying marketers

22.1   Marketers, publishers and owners of other media should ensure that marketing communications are designed and presented in such a way that it is clear that they are marketing communications. Unsolicited e-mail marketing communications should be clearly identifiable as marketing communications without the need to open them (see also cl 43.4c).

22.2   Distance-selling marketing communications should contain the full name of the marketers (and the suppliers if different).

Distance-selling marketing communications that require payment before products are received and have written response mechanisms should also contain the geographical address of the marketers (and the suppliers if different). Those that contain a telephone response mechanism only may contain the marketers' telephone number instead (though see cl 42.2a).

E-mail and mobile marketing communications should contain the full name and a valid address (eg, an e-mail address) of the marketers to which recipients can send opt-out requests.

Fax and non-live-sound automated-call marketing communications should contain the full name and a valid address or freephone number of the marketers to which recipients can send opt-out requests.

Sales promotions and marketing communications for one-day sales, homework schemes, business opportunities and the like should contain the full name and geographical address of the marketers (see cl 34.1h and s 52).

Marketing communications for employment agencies should contain the full name and contact details of the marketers.

The law requires marketers to identify themselves in some other marketing communications. Marketers should take legal advice.

Advertisement features

(see CAP Help Note on Advertisement Features)

23.1   Advertisement features, announcements or promotions, sometimes referred to as 'advertorials', that are disseminated in exchange for a payment or other reciprocal arrangement should comply with the Code if their content is controlled by the marketers rather than the publishers.

23.2   Marketers and publishers should make clear that advertisement features are advertisements, for example, by heading them 'advertisement feature'.

Free offers

24.1   See cll 32.1 to 32.3.

Notes: 25.0–26.0

Sales promotion rules

Introduction

27.1   The sales promotion rules must be read in conjunction with the general rules, direct marketing rules and other specific rules, if relevant.

27.2   The sales promotion rules are designed primarily to protect the public but they also apply to trade promotions and incentive schemes and to the promotional elements of sponsorships. They regulate the nature and administration of promotional marketing techniques. These techniques generally involve providing a range of direct or indirect additional benefits, usually on a temporary basis, designed to make goods or services more attractive to purchasers. The rules do not apply to the routine, non-promotional, distribution of products or to product extensions, for example, the suitability of one-off editorial supplements (be they in printed or electronic form) to newspapers and magazines.

27.3 Promoters are responsible for all aspects and all stages of promotions.

27.4 Promotions should be conducted equitably, promptly and efficiently and should be seen to deal fairly and honourably with consumers. Promoters should avoid causing unnecessary disappointment.

Protection of consumers, safety and suitability

28.1 Promoters should make all reasonable efforts to ensure that their promotions, including product samples, are safe and cause no harm to consumers or their property. Literature accompanying promotional items should give any necessary warnings and any appropriate safety advice.

28.2 Promoters should make every effort to ensure that unsuitable or inappropriate material does not reach consumers. Promotions should not be socially undesirable to the audience addressed by encouraging excessive consumption or inappropriate use and should be designed and conducted in a way that respects the right of consumers to a reasonable degree of privacy and freedom from annoyance.

28.3 No promotion or promotional item should cause serious or widespread offence to the audience addressed.

Children

29.1 Special care should be taken when promotions are addressed to children (people under 16) or when products intended for adults may fall into the hands of children.

29.2 Alcoholic drinks should not feature in promotions directed at people under 18.

Availability

30.1 Promoters should be able to demonstrate that they have made a reasonable estimate of likely response and that they were capable of meeting that response.

30.2   Phrases such as 'subject to availability' do not relieve promoters of the obligation to take all reasonable steps to avoid disappointing participants.

30.3   Promoters should not encourage consumers to make a purchase or series of purchases as a precondition to applying for promotional items if the number of those items is limited.

30.4   If promoters are unable to supply demand for a promotional offer because of an unexpectedly high response or some other unanticipated factor outside their control, they should offer refunds or substitute products in accordance with cl 42.5a.

30.5   When prize promotions are widely advertised, promoters should ensure that entry forms and any goods needed to establish proof of purchase are widely available.

Administration

31.1   Promotions should be conducted under proper supervision and adequate resources should be made available to administer them. Promoters and intermediaries should not give consumers justifiable grounds for complaint.

31.2   Promoters should allow adequate time for each phase of the promotion: notifying the trade, distributing the goods, issuing rules if relevant, collecting wrappers and the like, judging and announcing results.

31.3   Promoters should normally fulfil applications within 30 days in accordance with 42.4 and refund money in accordance with 42.5a.

Free offers and free trials

32.1   A free offer may be conditional on the purchase of other items. Consumers' liability for costs should be made clear in all material featuring the offer. An offer should be described as free only if consumers pay no more than:

a   the minimum, unavoidable cost of responding to the promotion, for example, the current public rates of postage, the cost of telephoning up to and including the national rate or the minimum, unavoidable cost of sending an e-mail or SMS text message b   the true cost of freight or delivery

c   the cost, including incidental expenses, of any travel involved if consumers collect the offer.

Promoters should not charge for packing, handling or administration.

32.2   Promoters must not try to recover their costs by reducing the quality or composition or by inflating the price of any product that must be bought as a pre-condition of obtaining the free item.

32.3   Promoters should not describe an individual element of a package as 'free' if the cost of that element is included in the package price.

32.4   Promoters should not use the term 'free trial' to describe 'satisfaction or your money back' offers, 'buy one get one free offers or other offers where a nonrefundable purchase is required. If appropriate, promoters should provide a cash refund, postal order or personal cheque promptly to free trial participants.

Prize promotions and the law

(see CAP Help Note on Promotions with Prizes)

33.1   Promotions with prizes including competitions, prize draws and instant win offers are subject to legal restrictions.

33.2   Promoters usually seek to avoid running illegal lotteries by running skill-based prize competitions (often using tiebreakers to identify the winners) or by offering free entry if the chance-based prize promotion might encourage purchase.

Promoters should take legal advice before embarking on such promotions.

Significant conditions for promotions

(see CAP Help Note on Promotions with Prizes)

34.1   Promotions should specify clearly before any purchase (or before or at the time of entry/application, if no purchase is required):

a   **How to participate**
how to participate, including significant conditions and costs, and any other major factors reasonably likely to influence consumers' decisions or understanding about the promotion

b   **Start date**
the start date, in any comparison referring to a special offer if the special offer has not yet begun

c   **Closing date**
a prominent closing date, if applicable, for purchases and submissions of entries/claims. Prize promotions and promotions addressed to or targeted at children always need a closing date. Some others do not, for example: comparisons that refer to a special offer (whether the promoter's previous offer or a competitor's offer), so long as they are and are stated to be 'subject to availability'; promotions limited only by the availability of promotional packs (eg, gifts with purchase, extra volume packs and reduced price packs); and loyalty schemes run on an open-ended basis.

Promoters must be able to demonstrate that the absence of a closing date will not disadvantage consumers. Promoters should state if the deadline for responding to undated promotional material will be calculated from the date the material was received by consumers. Closing dates should not be changed unless circumstances outside the reasonable control of the promoter make it unavoidable. If they are changed, promoters should take all reasonable steps to ensure that consumers who participated within the original terms are not disadvantaged.

d   **Proof of purchase**
any proof of purchase requirements. Prize promotions that might encourage, but do not require, purchase should state clearly that no purchase is necessary and should explain the free entry route

e   **Prizes**
the minimum number and nature of any prizes, if applicable. Promoters should state if prizes are to be awarded in instalments or are to be shared among recipients

f   **Restrictions**
geographical, personal or technological restrictions such as location, age or the need to have access to the Internet. Promoters should state any need to obtain permission to enter from an adult or employer

g **Availability of promotional packs**
where it is not obvious, if there is likely to be a limitation on the availability of promotional packs in relation to a stated closing date of the offer

h **Promoter's name and address**
the promoter's full name and business address, unless this is obvious from the context. Promotions by newspapers and magazines in their publications need not state the name and address if those can easily be found elsewhere in the publication

Participants should be able to retain the above conditions or have easy access to them throughout the promotion. Advertisements for promotions should specify all of the significant conditions above that are applicable.

Other rules for prize promotions

(see CAP Help Note on Promotions with Prizes)

35.1 Promoters should not claim that consumers have won a prize if they have not.

The distinction between prizes and gifts should always be clear. Gifts offered to all or most consumers in a promotion should not be described as prizes. If promoters offer gifts to all or most consumers in addition to giving prizes to those who win, particular care is needed to avoid confusing the two. In such cases, it should be clear that consumers 'qualify' for the gifts but have merely an opportunity to win the prizes. If promoters include a gift that consumers have qualified for in a list of other prizes, they should distinguish clearly between the two.

35.2 Promoters should not overstate consumers' chances of winning prizes. If promoters include consumers who have not won prizes in lists of those who have won prizes, they should distinguish clearly between the two.

35.3 Promoters should not claim that consumers are luckier than they are. They should not use terms such as 'finalist' or 'final stage' in a way that implies that consumers have progressed, by chance or skill, to an advanced stage of promotions if they have not.

35.4 Promoters should not claim that consumers must respond by a specified date or within a specified time if they need not.

35.5   Complex rules should be avoided and only very exceptionally will it be considered acceptable to supplement conditions of entry with additional rules.

If extra rules cannot be avoided, participants should be informed how to obtain them; the rules should contain nothing that could reasonably have influenced consumers against making a purchase or participating.

35.6   Withholding prizes can be justified only if participants have not met clear criteria set out in the promotional rules or if promoters have told consumers at the outset that insufficient entries or entries of insufficient quality will lead to the withholding of prizes.

35.7   Promoters of prize draws should ensure that prizes are awarded in accordance with the laws of chance and under the supervision of an independent observer.

35.8   Participants in instant win promotions should get their winnings at once or should know immediately what they have won and how to claim without delay, unreasonable costs or administrative barriers. Instant win tickets, tokens or numbers should be awarded on a fair and random basis and verification should take the form of an independently audited statement that all prizes have been distributed, or made available for distribution, in that manner.

35.9   Prize promotions should specify before or at the time of entry:

a   any restriction on the number of entries

b   whether or not a cash alternative can be substituted for any prize

c   when prizewinners will receive their prizes if later than six weeks after the closing date

d   how and when winners will be notified of results

e   how and when winners and results will be announced. Promoters should either publish or make available on request the name and county of major prize winners and, if applicable, their winning entries. Prize winners should not be compromised by the publication of excessively detailed personal information f   in a competition, ie, a game of skill or judgment, the criteria for judging entries (eg, the most apt and original tiebreaker). If the selection of winning entries is open to subjective interpretation, an independent judge, or a panel including one member who is independent of the competition's promoters and intermediaries, should be appointed. Those appointed to act as judges should be competent to judge the subject matter of the competition. The full names of judges should be made available on request

g   if relevant, who owns any copyright in the entries

h   if applicable, how entries will be returned by promoters

i   any intention to use winners in post-event publicity Participants should be able to retain the above conditions or have easy access to them throughout the promotion.

Front page flashes

(see CAP Help Note on Front Page Flashes)

36.1 Publishers announcing reader promotions on the front page or cover should ensure that consumers know whether they will be expected to buy subsequent editions of the publication. Major conditions that might reasonably influence consumers significantly in their decision to buy the publication should appear on the front page or cover.

Charity-linked promotions

(see CAP Help Note for Voluntary Sector Advertisers)

37.1 Promotions run by third parties (eg, commercial companies) claiming that participation will benefit registered charities or causes should:

a   name each charity or cause that will benefit and be able to show the ASA or CAP the formal agreement with those benefiting from the promotion

b   if it is not a registered charity, define its nature and objectives

c   specify exactly what will be gained by the named charity or cause and state the basis on which the contribution will be calculated d   state if the promoter has imposed a limit on its contributions

e   not limit consumers' contributions. If an amount is stated for each purchase, there should be no cut-off point for contributions. If a target total is stated, extra money collected should be given to the named charity or cause on the same basis as contributions below that level

f   be able to show that targets set are realistic

g   not exaggerate the benefit to the charity or cause derived from individual purchases of the promoted product

h   if asked, make available to consumers a current or final total of contributions made

i   take particular care when appealing to children (see cl 47.4e).

Trade incentives

38.1   Incentive schemes should be designed and implemented to take account of the interests of everyone involved and should not compromise the obligations of employees to give honest advice to consumers.

38.2   If promoters intend to ask for help from, or offer incentives to, another company's employees, they should require those employees to obtain their employer's permission before participating. Promoters should observe any procedures established by companies for their employees, including any rules for participating in promotions.

38.3   Incentive schemes should make clear to those benefiting that they may be responsible for paying tax.

Notes: 39–40

Direct marketing rules

41.1   The direct marketing rules must be read in conjunction with the general rules, sales promotion rules and other specific rules, if relevant. Moreover, the DMA also requires its members to observe the DMA Code of Practice. That code covers some practices (eg, telemarketing) that are not covered in this Code.

Distance selling

42.1 For the purposes of the Code, distance selling marketing communications are the final written advertised stage in the process that allows consumers to buy products without the buyer and seller meeting face-to-face. Marketers should comply with the Consumer Protection (Distance Selling) Regulations 2000.

Guidance on the legislation is available from www.dti.gov.uk. These clauses should be observed in conjunction with the legislation; they do not replace it.

42.2 Distance selling marketing communications should include:

a   for those communications that require payment before products are received and have written response mechanisms (eg, postal, fax or e-mail), the full name and geographical address of the marketers (and suppliers if different) outside the coupon or other response mechanism so that it can be retained by consumers. A separate address for orders may also be given; this need not be a full address but could, for example, be a Freepost address or a PO Box number.

Communications containing a telephone response mechanism only need merely state the full name and telephone number but consumers calling the number must be told the geographical address (and see 42.3d). Communications that do not require payment before products are received should state the full name of the marketers (and the suppliers if different)

b   the main characteristics of the products

c   the price, including any VAT or other taxes payable (see 15.2), and payment arrangements

d   the amount and number of any delivery charges

e   the estimated delivery/performance time (see 42.4) and arrangements

f   a statement that, unless inapplicable (see 42.6), consumers have the right to cancel orders for products. Marketers of services must state that the right to cancel will be lost once services have begun with the consumer's agreement, if they wish to limit consumers' cancellation rights in this way. They should, however, make it clear when the services will begin

g   any telephone, postal or other communication charges calculated at higher than the basic rate (eg, where a premium rate call is required)

h   any other limitation on the offer (eg, period of availability) and any other conditions that affect its validity

i   a statement as to whether marketers intend to provide substitute products (of equivalent quality and price) if those ordered are unavailable, and that they will meet the cost of returning substitute products on cancellation

j   the minimum duration of open-ended contracts; ie where goods are supplied or services performed permanently or recurrently.

42.3   At the latest by the time that goods are delivered or services begin, marketers should give consumers written information on:

a   unless inapplicable (see 42.6 below), how to exercise their right to cancel. Marketers should allow at least seven clear working days after delivery (or after the conclusion of service contracts) for consumers to cancel

b   in the case of goods, whether the consumer has to return the goods to the suppliers on cancellation and, if so, who is to bear the cost of return or recovery of the goods (though see 42.2i for substitute goods)

c   any other after-sales services and guarantees

d   the full geographical address of the suppliers for any consumer complaints

e   the conditions that apply to the cancellation of open-ended contracts.

42.4   Marketers should fulfil orders within 30 clear days from the day consumers send their orders unless they meet one of the following criteria and state the longer delivery time in the marketing communication: a longer delivery time might be given for products such as plants and made-to-measure products; marketers might make clear that they do not intend to begin production unless a sufficient response is received; or a series of products might be sent at regular intervals after the first 30 days.

42.5   Marketers must refund money promptly (and at the latest within 30 days of notice of cancellation being given) if:

a   consumers have not received products. If consumers prefer to wait they should be given a firm dispatch date or fortnightly progress reports. Alternatively marketers may, if asked or if stated before purchase, provide a substitute of equivalent quality and price

b   products are returned because they are damaged when received, are faulty or are not as described, in which case the marketers must bear the cost of transit in both directions

c   consumers cancel within seven clear working days after delivery (see 42.3a above). Consumers should assume they can try out products but should take reasonable care of them before they are returned (though see 42.6d). Consumers must return the products and pay the costs of doing so providing the marketers made this clear at the latest at the time the products were delivered (though see 42.2i for substitute goods)

d   an unconditional money-back guarantee is given and the products are returned within a reasonable period

e   products that have been returned are not received back, provided consumers can produce proof of posting.

42.6   So long as all contractual obligations to consumers are met, marketers do not have to provide a refund on:

a   services that have already begun, where 42.2f has been complied with

b   products the price of which is dependent on fluctuations in the financial market that are outside the control of the suppliers

c   perishable, personalised or made-to-measure products

d   audio or video recordings or computer software if unsealed by the consumer e   newspapers, periodicals or magazines

f   betting, gaming or lottery services.

42.7   If marketers intend to call on respondents personally, this should be made clear in the marketing communication or in a follow-up mailing. To allow consumers an adequate opportunity to refuse a personal visit, marketers should provide a reply-paid postcard or Freephone telephone contact instructions.

42.8   Marketers should take particular care when packaging products that might fall into the hands of children.

Database practice

43.1   Marketers should comply with all relevant data protection legislation. Guidance on this legislation is available from the Office of the Information Commissioner.

Although data protection legislation has a wide application, these clauses relate only to databases used for direct marketing purposes. The clauses should be observed in conjunction with the legislation; they do not replace it.

43.2   Marketers should take all necessary steps to ensure that:

a   marketing communications are suitable for those targeted

b   marketing communications are not sent unsolicited to consumers if explicit consent is required (see 43.4)

c   marketing communications are not sent to consumers who have asked not to receive them (see 43.9) or who have not had the opportunity to object to receiving them, if appropriate (see 43.3c). Those consumers should be identifiable

d   databases are accurate and up-to-date and, if rented, bought, etc, have been run against the most relevant suppression file operated by the relevant Preference Service. Reasonable requests for corrections to personal information should be acted upon within 60 days e   anyone who has been notified as dead is not mailed again and the notifier is referred to the relevant Preference Service

f   if asked in writing, consumers or the ASA (with consumers' consent) are given any information available on the nature and source of their personal details

Responsibility for complying with the above sub-clauses may not rest directly with marketers but with other data controllers. Those responsible will be expected to comply.

43.3   Except if it is obvious from the context, or if they already know, consumers should be informed at the time when personal information is collected:

a   who is collecting it (and the representative for data protection queries, if different)

b   why it is being collected

c   if it is intended to disclose the information to third parties, including associated but legally separate companies, or put the information to a use significantly different from that for which it is being provided, in which case an opportunity to prevent this should be given.

43.4   The explicit consent of consumers is required before:

a   processing sensitive personal data, including information on racial or ethnic origin, political opinion or religious or other similar beliefs, trade union membership, physical or mental health, sex life or any criminal record or allegation of criminal activity

b   sending marketing communications by fax. Explicit consent is not required when marketing by fax to corporate subscribers (see 1.3j), though marketers must comply with 43.2d in particular and, if necessary, run their databases against the fax data file

c   send marketing communications by e-mail or to mobile devices, save that marketers may send unsolicited marketing about their similar products to those whose details they have obtained in the course of, or in negotiations for, a sale. They should, however, tell them they may opt-out of future marketing both when they collect the data and on each occasion they send out marketing communications and should give them a simple means to do so. Explicit consent is not required when marketing business products to corporate subscribers (see 1.3j), including to their named employees

d   sending non-live-sound marketing communications by automated calling systems.

43.5   If after collection it is decided to use personal information for a purpose significantly different from that originally communicated, marketers should first get the explicit consent of consumers. Significantly different purposes include:

a   the disclosure of personal information to third parties for direct marketing purposes

b   the use or disclosure of personal information for any purpose substantially different from that which consumers could reasonably have foreseen and to which they might have objected.

43.6   The extent and detail of personal information held for any purpose should be adequate and relevant and should not be excessive for that purpose.

43.7   Personal information must always be held securely and should be safeguarded against unauthorised use, disclosure, alteration or destruction.

43.8   Personal information should not be kept for longer than is necessary for the purpose or purposes for which it was obtained.

43.9   Consumers are entitled to have their personal information suppressed. Enough information should be held by companies, though not for direct marketing purposes, to ensure that no further marketing communications are sent as a result of information about those consumers being re-obtained through a third party. If they want to reduce all unsolicited contact, consumers should register their names and contact details on all relevant suppression files.

43.10   Consumers who have asked for personal information about them to be suppressed may be contacted again if they ask to be reinstated.

43.11   Marketers are permitted to use published information that is generally available provided the consumer concerned is not listed on a relevant suppression file.

43.12 Any proposed transfer of a database to a country outside the European Economic Area should be made only if that country ensures an adequate level of protection for the rights and freedoms of consumers in relation to the processing of personal information or if contractual arrangements are in place to provide that protection.

Notes: 44–45

Other specific rules

Children

47.1 For the purposes of the Code, a child is someone under 16. The way in which children perceive and react to marketing communications is influenced by their age, experience and the context in which the message is delivered; marketing communications that are acceptable for young teenagers will not necessarily be acceptable for young children. The ASA will take these factors into account when assessing marketing communications.

47.2 Marketing communications addressed to, targeted at or featuring children should contain nothing that is likely to result in their physical, mental or moral harm:

a they should not be encouraged to enter strange places or talk to strangers. Care is needed when they are asked to make collections, enter schemes or gather labels, wrappers, coupons and the like

b they should not be shown in hazardous situations or behaving dangerously in the home or outside except to promote safety. Children should not be shown unattended in street scenes unless they are old enough to take responsibility for their own safety. Pedestrians and cyclists should be seen to observe the Highway Code

c they should not be shown using or in close proximity to dangerous substances or equipment without direct adult supervision. Examples include matches, petrol, certain medicines and household substances as well as certain electrical appliances and machinery, including agricultural equipment

d they should not be encouraged to copy any practice that might be unsafe for a child.

47.3   Marketing communications addressed to, targeted at or featuring children should not exploit their credulity, loyalty, vulnerability or lack of experience:

a   they should not be made to feel inferior or unpopular for not buying the advertised product

b   they should not be made to feel that they are lacking in courage, duty or loyalty if they do not buy or do not encourage others to buy a particular product

c   it should be made easy for them to judge the size, characteristics and performance of any product advertised and to distinguish between real-life situations and fantasy

d   adult permission should be obtained before they are committed to purchasing complex and costly products.

47.4   Marketing communications addressed to or targeted at children:

a   should not actively encourage them to make a nuisance of themselves to parents or others and should not undermine parental authority

b   should not make a direct appeal to purchase unless the product is one that would be likely to interest children and that they could reasonably afford. Distance selling marketers should take care when using youth media not to promote products that are unsuitable for children

c   should not exaggerate what is attainable by an ordinary child using the product being marketed

d   should not actively encourage them to eat or drink at or near bedtime, to eat frequently throughout the day or to replace main meals with confectionery or snack foods

e   should not exploit their susceptibility to charitable appeals and should explain the extent to which their participation will help in any charity-linked promotions.

47.5   Promotions addressed to or targeted at children:

a   should not encourage excessive purchases in order to participate b should make clear that adult permission is required if prizes and incentives might cause conflict. Examples include animals, bicycles, tickets for outings, concerts and holidays

c should clearly explain the number and type of any additional proofs of purchase needed to participate

d should contain a prominent closing date

e should not exaggerate the value of prizes or the chances of winning them.

Motoring

48.1 Marketing communications for motor vehicles, fuel or accessories should avoid portraying or referring to practices that encourage or condone anti-social behaviour.

48.2 Marketers should not make speed or acceleration claims the predominant message of their marketing communications. However it is legitimate to give general information about a vehicle's performance such as acceleration and mid-range statistics, braking power, road-holding and top speed.

48.3 Marketers should not portray speed in a way that might encourage motorists to drive irresponsibly or to break the law and should not condone irresponsible driving.

48.4 Vehicles should not be depicted in dangerous or unwise situations in a way that might encourage or condone irresponsible driving. Their capabilities may be demonstrated on a track or circuit provided it is clearly not in use as a public highway.

48.5 Care should be taken in cinema commercials and those in electronic media where the moving image may give the impression of excessive speed. In all cases where vehicles are shown in normal driving circumstances on public roads they should be seen not to exceed UK speed limits.

48.6 When making environmental claims for their products, marketers should conform with the rules on Environmental Claims.

48.7 Prices quoted should correspond to the vehicles illustrated. For example, it is not acceptable to feature only a top-of-the-range model alongside the starting price for that range.

48.8   Safety claims should not exaggerate the benefit to consumers. Marketers should not make absolute claims about safety unless they hold evidence to support them.

Environmental claims

(See CAP Help Note on Claims for Organic Food)

49.1   The basis of any claim should be explained clearly and should be qualified where necessary. Unqualified claims can mislead if they omit significant information.

49.2   Claims such as 'environmentally friendly' or 'wholly biodegradable' should not be used without qualification unless marketers can provide convincing evidence that their product will cause no environmental damage when taking into account the full life cycle of the product. Qualified claims and comparisons such as 'greener' or 'friendlier' may be acceptable if marketers can substantiate that their product provides an overall improvement in environmental terms either against their competitors' or their own previous products.

49.3   Where there is a significant division of scientific opinion or where evidence is inconclusive this should be reflected in any statements made in the marketing communication. Marketers should not suggest that their claims command universal acceptance if that is not the case.

49.4   If a product has never had a demonstrably adverse effect on the environment, marketing communications should not imply that the formulation has changed to make it safe. It is legitimate, however, to make claims about a product whose composition has changed or has always been designed in a way that omits chemicals known to cause damage to the environment.

49.5   The use of extravagant language should be avoided, as should bogus and confusing scientific terms. If it is necessary to use a scientific expression, its meaning should be clear.

Health and beauty products and therapies

(see CAP Help Notes, particularly those on: Substantiation for Health, Beauty and Slimming Claims; Health, Beauty and Slimming Advertisements that Refer to Ailments; and Use of Experts by the ASA and CAP)

General

50.1 Medical and scientific claims made about beauty and health-related products should be backed by evidence, where appropriate consisting of trials conducted on people. Where relevant, the rules will also relate to claims for products for animals. Substantiation will be assessed by the ASA on the basis of the available scientific knowledge.

50.2 Marketers inviting consumers to diagnose their own minor ailments should not make claims that might lead to a mistaken diagnosis.

50.3 Marketers should not discourage essential treatment. They should not offer specific advice on, diagnosis of or treatment for serious or prolonged conditions unless it is conducted under the supervision of a doctor or other suitably qualified health professional (eg, one subject to regulation by a statutory or recognised medical or health professional body). Accurate and responsible general information about such conditions may, however, be offered.

50.4 Consumers should not be encouraged to use products to excess and marketers should hold proof before suggesting their products or therapies are guaranteed to work, absolutely safe or without side-effects.

50.5 Marketing communications should not suggest that any product is safe or effective merely because it is 'natural' or that it is generally safer because it omits an ingredient in common use.

50.6 Marketers offering individual treatments, particularly those that are physically invasive, may be asked by the media and the ASA to provide full details together with information about those who will supervise and administer them.

Where appropriate, practitioners should have relevant and recognised qualifications. Marketers should encourage consumers to take independent medical advice before committing themselves to significant treatments, including those that are physically invasive.

50.7 References to the relief of symptoms or the superficial signs of ageing are acceptable if they can be substantiated. Unqualified claims such as 'cure' and 'rejuvenation' are not generally acceptable.

50.8 Marketers should hold proof before claiming or implying that minor addictions and bad habits can be treated without effort from those suffering.

50.9   Marketers should not use unfamiliar scientific words for common conditions.

Medicines

50.10   The Medicines Act 1968 and its regulations, as well as regulations implementing European Community Directive 92/28/EEC, govern the advertising and promotion of medicines and the conditions of ill health that they can be offered to treat. Guidance on the legislation is available from the Medicines Control Agency (MCA).

50.11   Medicines must have a marketing authorisation from the MCA before they are marketed and any claims made for products must conform with the authorisation. Medicinal claims should not be made for unauthorised products.

Marketing communications should refer to the MCA, the authorisation or the EC only if required to do so by the MCA.

50.12   Prescription-only medicines may not be advertised to the public. Health-related claims in marketing communications addressed only to the medical, dental, veterinary and allied professions are exempt from the Code.

50.13   Marketing communications should include the name of the product, an indication of what it is for, text such as 'Always read the label' and the common name of the active ingredient if there is only one. There should be no suggestion that any medicine is either a food or a cosmetic.

50.14   Marketers must not use fear or anxiety to promote medicines or recovery from illness and should not suggest that using or avoiding a product can affect normal good health.

50.15   Illustrations of the effect or action of any product should be accurate.

50.16   Marketing communications for medicines should not be addressed to children.

50.17   Marketers should not use health professionals or celebrities to endorse medicines.

50.18   Marketing communications for any medicine should not claim that its effects are as good as or better than those of another identifiable product.

50.19 Homeopathic medicinal products must be registered in the United Kingdom. Any product information given in the marketing communication should be confined to what appears on the label. Marketing communications should include a warning to consult a doctor if symptoms persist. Marketing communications for unauthorised products should not make any medicinal or therapeutic claims or refer to any ailment.

Vitamins, minerals and other food supplements

50.20 Marketers should hold scientific evidence for any claim that their vitamin or mineral product or other food supplement is beneficial to health. In assessing claims the ASA and CAP will bear in mind recommendations made by bodies such as the Department of Health and the Food Standards Agency.

50.21 A well-balanced diet should provide the vitamins and minerals needed each day by a normal, healthy individual. Marketers may offer vitamin and mineral supplements to certain groups as a safeguard to help maintain good health but should not imply that they can be used to prevent or treat illness, elevate mood or enhance normal performance. Without well-established proof, no marketing communication should suggest that there is widespread vitamin or mineral deficiency or that it is necessary or therapeutic to augment a well-balanced diet. Individuals should not be encouraged to swap a healthy diet for supplementation.

50.22 People who are potentially at risk of deficiency may be safeguarded by vitamin and mineral supplementation. Products must be appropriate and marketing communications should specify the group they are addressing when claiming or implying that health may be maintained. Indicative groups include:

a   people who eat nutritionally inadequate meals

b   the elderly

c   children and adolescents

d   convalescents

e   athletes in training or others who are physically very active

f   women of child-bearing age

g　lactating and pregnant women

h　people on restricted food or energy diets

i　people with Asian ancestry from the Indian sub-continent

j　people who smoke.

50.23　Serious vitamin and mineral depletion caused by illness should be diagnosed and treated by a doctor. Self-medication should not be promoted on the basis that it will influence the speed or extent of recovery.

Cosmetics

50.24　Claims made about the action that a cosmetic has on or in the skin should distinguish between the composition of the product and any effects brought about by the way in which it is applied, such as massage. Scientific evidence should also make this distinction.

50.25　Some cosmetics have an effect on the kind of skin changes that are caused by environmental factors. Marketing communications for them can therefore refer to temporarily preventing, delaying or masking premature ageing.

Hair and scalp

50.26　Marketers should be able to provide scientific evidence, where appropriate in the form of trials conducted on people, for any claim that their product or therapy can prevent baldness or slow it down, arrest or reverse hair loss, stimulate or improve hair growth, nourish hair roots, strengthen the hair or improve its health as distinct from its appearance.

Weight control

(see CAP Slimming Guidelines for Press Advertisements)

51.1　A weight reduction regime in which the intake of energy is lower than its output is the most common self-treatment for achieving weight reduction. Any claims made for the effectiveness or action of a weight reduction method or product should be backed if appropriate by rigorous trials on people; testimonials that are not supported by trials do not constitute substantiation.

51.2   Obesity in adults is defined by a body mass index (BMI) of more than 30 kg/m2. Obesity is frequently associated with medical conditions and treatments for it should not be advertised to the public unless they are to be used under suitably qualified supervision.

51.3   Marketing communications for any weight reduction regime or establishment should neither be directed at, nor contain anything that will appeal particularly to, people who are under 18 or those in whom weight reduction would produce a potentially harmful body weight (BMI of less than 18.5 kg/m2). Marketing communications should not suggest that it is desirable to be underweight.

51.4   Marketers must show that weight reduction is achieved by loss of body fat before claims are made for a weight reduction aid or regimen. Combining a diet with an unproven weight reduction method does not justify making weight reduction claims for that method.

51.5   Marketers should be able to show that their diet plans are nutritionally wellbalanced (except for producing a deficit of energy) and this should be assessed in relation to the kind of person who would be using them.

51.6   Vitamins and minerals do not contribute to weight reduction but may be offered to slimmers as a safeguard against any shortfall when dieting.

51.7   Marketers promoting Very Low Calorie Diets and other diets that fall below 800 calories a day should do so only for short term use and should encourage users to take medical advice before embarking on them. Marketers should also have regard to the voluntary code of practice in the COMA report 'The Use of Very Low Energy Diets' (1987).

51.8   Marketing communications for diet aids should make clear how they work. Prominence must be given to the role of the diet and marketing communications should not give the impression that dieters cannot fail or can eat as much as they like and still lose weight.

51.9   Marketing communications should not contain claims that people can lose precise amounts of weight within a stated period or that weight or fat can be lost from specific parts of the body.

51.10   Claims that individuals have lost exact amounts of weight should be compatible with good medical and nutritional practice, should state the period involved and should not be based on unrepresentative experiences. For those who are normally overweight, a rate of weight loss greater than 2 lbs (just under 1 kg) per week is unlikely to be compatible with good medical and nutritional practice. For those who are obese, a rate of weight loss greater than 2 lbs per week in the early stages of dieting may be compatible with good medical and nutritional practice.

51.11   Resistance and aerobic exercise can improve muscular condition and tone; this can improve body shape and posture. Marketers should be able to substantiate any claims that such methods used alone or in conjunction with a diet plan can lead to weight or inch reduction. Marketing communications for intensive exercise programmes should encourage users to check with a doctor before starting.

51.12   Short-term loss of girth may be achieved by wearing a tight-fitting garment. This should not be portrayed as permanent, nor should it be confused with weight or fat reduction.

Employment and business opportunities

52.1   Marketers should distinguish clearly between offers of employment and business opportunities. Before publication, media normally require full details of the marketers and any terms and conditions imposed on respondents.

52.2   Employment marketing communications must correspond to genuine vacancies and potential employees must not be asked to send money for further details. Living and working conditions should not be misrepresented.

Quoted earnings should be precise; if a forecast has to be made this should not be unrepresentative. If income is earned from a basic salary and commission, commission only, or in some other way, this should be made clear.

52.3   An employment agency must make clear in marketing communications its full name and contact details and, if the name does not disclose that fact, that it is an employment agency.

52.4   Marketing communications for homework schemes requiring participants to make articles, perform services or offer facilities at or from home should contain:

a   the full name and geographical address of the marketers

b   a clear description of the work; the support available to home-workers should not be exaggerated

c   an indication of whether participants are self-employed or employed by a business

d   the likely level of earnings, but only if this can be supported with evidence of the experience of current homeworkers

e   no forecast of earnings if the scheme is new

f   a statement of any required investment or binding obligation

g   a statement of any charges for raw materials, machines, components, administration and the like

h   information on whether the marketers will buy back any products made

i   any limitations or conditions that might influence consumers prior to their decision to participate.

Marketers may include that information in follow-up literature made available to all consumers before commitment but the initial marketing communication should state if a financial outlay is required.

52.5 Marketing communications for business opportunities should contain:

a   the full name and geographical address of the marketers

b   a clear description of the work involved and the extent of investors' commitments, including any financial investment; the support available should not be exaggerated

c   no unrepresentative or exaggerated earnings figures.

Marketers may include that information in follow-up literature made available to all consumers before commitment but the initial marketing communication should normally state if an investment is required.

52.6   Marketing communications for vocational training and other instruction courses should make no promises of employment unless it is guaranteed. The duration of the course and the level of attainment needed to embark on it should be made clear.

52.7   Marketing communications for the sale of directories giving details of employment or business opportunities should indicate plainly the nature of what is being offered.

Financial products

53.1   Marketers must have regard to the Financial Services and Markets Act 2000 and the Financial Services and Markets Act 2000 (Financial Promotion) Order 2005, both enforced by the Financial Services Authority (FSA), and also to other rules and relevant guidance issued by the FSA. The scope of that legislation and guidance extends to marketing communications for: investments and investment advice; deposit taking (eg, banking); general insurance and pure protection policies (eg, term assurance). The FSA is responsible for the regulation of first charge mortgage lending and selling, as well as certain secured loans and the activities of insurance intermediaries. The FSA does not provide pre-publication advice on proposed financial marketing communications. Technical guidance is available on specific matters or rule interpretation only. For more information contact the FSA Financial Promotions Review and Remediation Team (see www.fsa.gov.uk).

The OFT will continue to regulate other consumer loans under the Consumer Credit Act 1974 (as amended).

The rules that follow apply to financial marketing communications that are not regulated by the FSA or OFT. All financial marketing communications are, however, subject to Code clauses that cover 'non-technical' elements of communications, for example, serious or widespread offence, social responsibility and the truthfulness of claims that do not relate to specific characteristics of financial products.

53.2   Offers of financial products should be set out in a way that allows them to be understood easily by the audience being addressed. Marketers should ensure that they do not take advantage of people's inexperience or credulity.

53.3   Marketing communications should state the nature of the contract being withdrawal. Alternatively, if a marketing communication is short or general in its content, free explanatory material giving full details of the offer should be readily available before a binding contract is entered into.

53.4 The basis used to calculate any rates of interest, forecasts or projections should be apparent immediately.

53.5 Marketing communications should make clear that the value of investments is variable and, unless guaranteed, can go down as well as up. If the value of the investment is guaranteed, details should be included in the marketing communication.

53.6 Marketing communications should make clear that past performance or experience does not necessarily give a guide for the future. Any examples used should not be unrepresentative.

Betting and gaming

54.1 The gaming industry and the advertising business accept responsibility for ensuring that marketing communications contain nothing that is likely to lead people to adopt styles of gambling that are unwise.

54.2 Marketing communications should be socially responsible and should not encourage excessive gambling.

54.3 Care should be taken not to exploit the young, the immature or those who are mentally or socially vulnerable.

54.4 Marketing communications should not be directed at people under 18 through the selection of media, style of presentation, content or context in which they appear. No medium should be used to advertise betting and gaming if more than 25 per cent of its audience is under 18 years of age.

54.5 People shown gambling should not be, nor should they look, under 25.

Casinos

54.6 Licensed casinos can only use classified advertisements to advertise to the public. Such advertisements should be restricted to the name, logo, address, telephone and fax numbers of the premises, factual information about ownership, the facilities provided, those who may be admitted and how to apply for membership.

54.7   Marketing material other than classified may be sent only to the members of such casinos.

Tobacco, rolling papers and filters

55.1   The previous edition of this Code contained strict rules (The Cigarette Code) that applied to marketing communications for tobacco products (cigarettes and hand-rolling tobacco), rolling papers and filters. The Cigarette Code was exceptional in that it was the outcome of discussions between the Department of Health, the manufacturers and importers of cigarettes (represented by the Tobacco Manufacturers' Association and the Imported Tobacco Products Advisory Council respectively) and the ASA. It ran in parallel with, and its rules were applied in addition to, those imposed elsewhere in the Codes.

The Tobacco Advertising and Promotion Act 2002 now prohibits the advertising of tobacco products. It does not, however, cover advertisements for rolling papers or filters and does permit certain tobacco advertising at point of sale.

Self-regulatory rules and procedures for these categories are under review and will be published on www.cap.org.uk when finalised.

Self-regulatory rules covering the marketing of rolling papers and filters were published on 30 October 2003 and appear below.

Rules Covering the Marketing of Rolling Papers and Filters

Introduction

1.1   Past editions of the British Codes of Advertising and Sales Promotion contained strict rules (the Cigarette Code) that applied to marketing communications for tobacco products (cigarettes and hand-rolling tobacco), rolling papers and filters. The Cigarette Code was exceptional in that it was the outcome of discussions between the Department of Health, the manufacturers and importers of cigarettes (represented by the Tobacco Manufacturers' Association and the Imported Tobacco Products Advisory Council ITPAC respectively) and the ASA. It ran in parallel with, and its rules were applied in addition to, those imposed elsewhere in the Codes.

1.2   The Tobacco Advertising and Promotion Act 2002 prohibits the advertising of tobacco products. It does not, however, cover marketing communications for rolling papers or filters and permitted certain tobacco advertising at point of sale.

1.3 Edition 11 of the British Code of Advertising, Sales Promotion and Direct Marketing (the CAP Code) states that self-regulatory rules and procedures for the categories in 1.2 above are under review and will be published on www.cap.org.uk when finalised.

Scope

2.1 This document contains the rules covering the non-broadcast marketing of rolling papers and filters. They have been drawn up by CAP, the ASA and the manufacturers and importers of rolling papers and filters. They run in parallel with, and are applied in addition to, the rules imposed elsewhere in the CAP Code

2.2 The rules govern the content of marketing communications (see cll 1.1 and 1.2 of the CAP Code), including point of sale material, for the following:

a   rolling papers and filters

b   any product, if the marketing communication concerned features rolling papers, filters or pack designs of a recognisable brand available in the United Kingdom

c   products displaying the colours, livery, insignia or name of a rolling paper or brand of filter in a way that promotes smoking rather than these branded products.

2.3 The rules do not apply to marketing communications:

a   addressed to the trade in its professional capacity in media not targeted at the public

b   for schemes, events or activities sponsored or financially supported by manufacturers or importers, including sports sponsorship, so long as undue emphasis is not placed on the rolling papers or filters as opposed to the scheme, event or activity

c   on manufacturers' or importers' own websites (subject to 1.2q of the CAP Code). Other rules in the CAP Code, for example, the sales promotion rules, may apply to 2.3 a and b above.

2.4   The rules are not intended to hamper fair competition. Marketers of rolling papers and filters are free to attract attention to their products, provided both the spirit and the letter of the rules are observed.

2.5   Claims encompass statements and visual presentations and can be direct or indirect. Claims which the ASA or CAP regard as eroding or diminishing the effectiveness of the rules will be judged contrary to the spirit of the rules. Humour is acceptable provided it is used with care and is not likely to have a particular appeal to the young.

2.6   The ASA is the final arbiter of the meaning of the rules. The CAP Copy Advice team provides advice on whether marketing is likely to break the rules. Marketers are urged to check their marketing communications with the CAP Copy Advice team before publishing them. Point of sale material featuring executions, themes or elements already checked for other marketingcommunications should normally need no additional checking by CAP.

2.7   When interpreting the rules, the Copy Advice team and the ASA will make due allowance for the medium in which the marketing communication is to appear, the audience and its likely response.

Rules

3.1   No marketing communications should depict anyone smoking.

3.2   Marketing communications should not encourage people to start smoking.

3.3   Marketing communications should not encourage smokers to increase their consumption or smoke to excess.

3.4   Marketing communications should not be targeted at, or be likely to appeal to, people under 18. Anyone depicted in marketing communications should always be, and clearly be seen to be, over 25. No medium should be used to market rolling papers or filters if more than 25 per cent of its audience is under 18 or women under 24.

3.5   Marketing communications should not play on the susceptibilities of those who are physically or emotionally vulnerable, particularly the young or immature.

3.6   Marketing communications should not encourage or condone the use of illegal drugs. Save in exceptional circumstances, for example, in the context of an anti-drug message, any reference to illegal drugs will be regarded as condoning their use.

3.7   Marketing communications should not be sexually titillating.

3.8   Marketing communications should not imply that smoking is glamorous or aspirational or that it enhances people's femininity, masculinity or appearance. Nor should they imply that smoking leads to social, sexual, romantic or business success. In particular, marketing communications should not link smoking with people who are evidently well-known, wealthy, fashionable, sophisticated or successful or who possess other attributes or qualities that may reasonably be expected to command admiration or encourage emulation.

3.9   Marketing communications should not appeal to the adventurous or rebellious, imply that it is daring to smoke or imply that smoking enhances people's independence.

3.10   Marketing communications should not imply that smoking is safe, healthy, natural, popular or appropriate in all circumstances. Marketing communications should not suggest that smoking promotes relaxation or concentration, through references to people smoking when they are relaxing or concentrating may be acceptable. Marketing communications should avoid any suggestion of a healthy or wholesome lifestyle and should not associate smoking with healthy eating and drinking, sport or active/outdoor games.

Alcoholic drinks

(See the CAP Help Note on Health, Diet and Nutritional Claims in Marketing Communications for Alcoholic Drinks)

56.1   For the purposes of the Code, alcoholic drinks are those that exceed 1.2 per cent alcohol by volume.

56.2   Marketing communications must contain nothing that is likely to lead people to adopt styles of drinking that are unwise. Alcohol must not be handled or served irresponsibly. The consumption of alcohol may be portrayed as sociable and thirst-quenching. Marketing communications may be humorous but must nevertheless conform with the intention of the rules.

56.3

a   As is implied by cl 2.8, the spirit as well as the letter of the rules in this section apply whether or not a product is shown or referred to or seen being consumed.

b   The rules are not intended to inhibit advertising on alcohol-related health or safety themes that is responsible and is not likely to promote a brand of alcohol

56.4   Marketing communications should be socially responsible and should neither encourage excessive drinking nor suggest that drinking can overcome boredom, loneliness or other problems. They should not suggest that alcohol might be indispensable. Care should be taken not to exploit the young, the immature or those who are mentally or socially vulnerable.

56.5   Marketing communications should not be directed at people under 18 through the selection of media, style of presentation, content or context in which they appear. No medium should be used to advertise alcoholic drinks if more than 25 per cent of its audience is under 18 years.

56.6   People shown drinking or playing a significant role should neither be nor look under 25 and should not be shown behaving in an adolescent or juvenile way. Younger people may be shown in marketing communications, for example in the context of family celebrations, but should be obviously not drinking.

56.7   Marketing communications should not be associated with people under 18 or reflect their culture. They should not feature or portray real or fictitious characters who are likely to appeal particularly to people under 18 in a way that might encourage them to drink.

56.8   Marketing communications should not suggest that any alcoholic drink has therapeutic qualities (eg, stimulant or sedative qualities) or can change moods or enhance confidence, mental or physical capabilities or performance, popularity or sporting achievements. They should not link alcoholic drinks to illicit drugs.

56.9   Marketing communications must neither link alcohol with seduction, sexual activity or sexual success nor imply that alcohol can enhance attractiveness, masculinity or femininity.

56.10   Marketing communications may give factual information about the alcoholic strength of a drink or make factual strength comparisons with other products but must not otherwise suggest that a drink may be preferred because of its high alcohol content or intoxicating effect. Drinks may be presented as preferable because of low or lower strength.

56.11 Marketing communications should not suggest that drinking alcohol is a reason for the success of any personal relationship or social event. A brand preference may be promoted as a mark of, for example, the drinker's good taste and discernment.

56.12 Drinking alcohol should not be portrayed as a challenge, especially to the young. Marketing communications should neither show, imply or refer to aggression or unruly, irresponsible or anti-social behaviour nor link alcohol with brave, tough or daring people or behaviour.

56.13 Particular care should be taken to ensure that marketing communications for sales promotions requiring multiple purchases do not encourage excessive consumption.

56.14 Marketing communications should not depict activities or locations in which drinking alcohol would be unsafe or unwise. In particular, marketing communications should not associate the consumption of alcohol with an occupation that requires concentration to be done safely, for example, operating machinery, driving or activity relating to water or heights. Alcohol should not normally be shown in a work environment.

Low alcohol drinks

56.15 Low alcohol drinks are those that contain between 0.5per cent to 1.2 per cent alcohol by volume. Marketers should ensure that low alcohol drinks are not promoted in a way that encourages their inappropriate consumption and should not depict activities that require complete sobriety.

How the system works

The self-regulatory system

60.1 The self-regulatory system comprises three bodies: the Advertising Standards Authority (ASA), the Advertising Standards Board of Finance (ASBOF) and the CAP. Their work is described below.

60.2   The strength of the system depends on the long-term commitment of all those involved in advertising, sales promotions and direct marketing (marketing). Practitioners in every sphere share an interest in seeing that marketing communications are welcomed and trusted by their audience; unless they are accepted and believed they cannot succeed. If they are offensive or misleading they discredit everyone associated with them and the industry as a whole.

60.3   The Code and all ASA rulings together with ASA and CAP guidance on a wide range of topics are available on www.asa.org.uk and www.cap.org.uk. The ASA and CAP update their websites regularly. The Executive provides an information hotline between 9.00am and 5.30pm Mon–Fri on 020 7580 5555. For copy advice from CAP ring 020 7580 4100/ fax 020 7580 4072/e-mail copyadvice@cap.org.uk/ visit www.cap.org.uk.

The ASA

60.4   The ASA was established in 1962 to provide independent scrutiny of the newly created self-regulatory system set up by the industry. Its chief tasks are to promote and enforce high standards in marketing communications, to investigate complaints, to identify and resolve problems through its own research, to ensure that the system operates in the public interest and to act as the channel for communications with those who have an interest in marketing communication standards.

60.5   The ASA is a limited company and is independent of both the Government and the marketing business. The Chairman of the ASA is appointed by ASBOF and is unconnected with the marketing business. A majority of the current 12-member Council appointed by the Chairman to govern the ASA is also unconnected with the marketing business. All Council members sit as individuals and are selected, as far as possible, to reflect a diversity of background and experience. Vacancies for independent members of Council are publicly advertised. Members serve for a maximum of two- to three-year terms.

60.6   The ASA investigates complaints from any source against marketing communications in non-broadcast media. Marketers are told the outcome of the ASA Council's rulings and, where appropriate, are asked to withdraw or amend their marketing communications. The adjudications reached by the Council are published weekly on www.asa.org.uk.

60.7   The ASA gives equal emphasis to conducting a substantial research and monitoring programme by reviewing issues and marketing communications that fall within its scope. Particular media and product categories may be identified for scrutiny. In this way the ASA can identify trends and prevent future problems.

60.8   Publicising the ASA's policies and actions is essential to sustaining wide acceptance of the system's integrity. A comprehensive programme of seminars and speeches, advertising, leaflets, briefing notes on a wide range of topics, a video targeted at consumers and educational establishments, articles written for professional journals, newspaper, magazine, TV and radio coverage all augment the ASA's extensive media presence.

The ASBOF

60.9   The ASBOF sets the framework for industry policy making and is responsible for the CAP and for funding the self-regulatory system.

60.10   The self-regulatory system is funded principally by a levy on advertising and direct marketing expenditure collected by ASBOF. This separation of operation and responsibilities helps to ensure that the independent judgment of the ASA is not compromised.

60.11   ASBOF's members are advertisers, promoters and direct marketers, their agencies, the media and the trade and professional organisations of the advertising, sales promotion and direct marketing businesses.

The CAP

60.12   CAP's role is to ensure that marketing communications within the Code's remit that are commissioned, prepared, placed or published in the UK conform with the rules in the British Code of Advertising, Sales Promotion and Direct Marketing.

60.13   CAP co-ordinates the activities of its members to achieve the highest degree of compliance with the Code. It creates, reviews and amends the Code. From time to time, it produces for the industry Help Notes that give detailed guidance on specific sectors or subjects that are covered only generally in the Code. It oversees the sanctions operated by its members. It operates a website, www.cap.org.uk, to provide information and guidance to the industry, including access to all Help Notes and relevant Ad Alerts. It convenes ad hoc Working

Groups for limited periods to address specific subjects arising out of the selfregulatory process.

60.14   The Code establishes a standard against which marketing communications are assessed. Additional codes exist in many other sectors; where appropriate these require practitioners to conform with the CAP Code.

60.15   The Chairman of CAP works on a part-time basis and is appointed for an agreed period and remunerated by ASBOF.

60.16   CAP actively encourages participation in the self-regulatory system. Suggestions for improving the Code's rules or modifying their application should be sent in writing to the Chairman. If changes are adopted by CAP their introduction is normally deferred for a short time to give marketers an adequate opportunity to amend their marketing communications.

The CAP Copy Advice team

60.17   The CAP Copy Advice team gives advice to marketers, their agencies, the media and others on the likely conformity with the Code of marketing communications before they are published or distributed. In addition, it checks marketing communications produced by marketers subject to mandatory prevetting (for example, those subject to the poster pre-vetting sanction). Copy advice is free and confidential from competitors. The vast majority of written enquiries are dealt with within 24 hours although lengthy submissions may take longer, particularly those that include detailed evidence that needs to be reviewed by external expert consultants. Favourable pre-publication advice does not automatically protect marketers from complaints being investigated and upheld by the ASA. It is, however, a highly authoritative guide to what is likely to comply with the Code. Advice on the most common issues is available by accessing the AdviceOnline database on www.cap.org.uk. AdviceOnline is updated regularly by the Copy Advice team.

The CAP Compliance team

60.18   The CAP Compliance team ensures that marketing communications conform with the Code to protect consumers and ensure a level playing-field. It enforces ASA decisions in individual cases and when a decision has ramifications for a whole sector. It takes action against marketers who persistently break the Code. In exceptional cases where a clear breach of the Code is evident, for example, if a marketing communication contains claims that are blatantly misleading, the team takes immediate compliance action to stop the obviously problematic marketing communications from reappearing. On occasion, that compliance action is taken while an ASA investigation proceeds (see 60.35 and 61.3).

The team co-ordinates the sanctions operated by the Executive and by CAP members; in particular it issues Ad Alerts to CAP members, including the media, advising them to withhold their services from non-compliant marketers or deny those marketers access to advertising space.

Information on compliance is available on www.cap.org.uk. Companies that are members of a CAP trade association or professional body can access a database of relevant Ad Alerts on a secure section of the CAP website.

The CAP Panels

60.19 Much of the detailed work of CAP is done by its two Panels. The Sales Promotion and Direct Response Panel concentrates on sales promotions and direct marketing. The General Media Panel concentrates on all other marketing, media and related issues. Each Panel is composed of industry experts together with one ASA Council member.

The Panels guide the Executive and help the ASA and CAP to produce advice for the industry and to interpret the Code both in individual cases and on general issues.

The Panels also provide a forum to reassess recommendations and advice given by the Executive. The Panels can be asked to look at an issue by the parties to a complaint before the ASA Council has adjudicated; Council will take account of the Panels' opinions. Council's judgment on the interpretation of the Code is, however, final. Anyone directly affected by copy advice given by the Executive on behalf of CAP can ask for it to be considered by the relevant Panel. The Panel Chairmen can reject requests and will do so if it appears that the Panels are being used to hamper the effective running of the self-regulatory system.

The administration of the system

60.20   The ASA and CAP share a joint Executive whose duties are organised to recognise the distinct functions of the two bodies. The Executive carries out the day-to-day work of the system and acts as a channel of communication, ensuring that industry expertise, specialist advice and the decisions of the ASA Council are co-ordinated and disseminated. The ASA Council and CAP form an independent judgment on any matter reported to them after they have considered the Executive's recommendations.

60.21   Marketers bear principal responsibility for the marketing communications they produce and must be able to prove the truth of their claims to the ASA; they have a duty to make their claims fair and honest and to avoid causing serious or widespread offence. Agencies have an obligation to create marketing communications that are accurate, ethical and neither mislead nor cause serious or widespread offence. Publishers and media owners recognise that they should disseminate only those marketing communications that conform with the Code. This responsibility extends to any other agent involved in producing, placing or publishing marketing communications. They accept the rulings of the ASA Council as binding.

60.22   The ASA Council judges whether marketing communications are contrary to the Code. Everyone responsible for commissioning, preparing, placing and publishing a marketing communication that breaches the Code will be asked to act promptly to amend or withdraw it.

The law

60.23   Marketers, agencies and publishers have primary responsibility for ensuring that everything they do is legal. Since the first Code was published the number of laws designed to protect consumers has greatly increased. There are directives emanating from the European Community as well as more than 200 UK statutes, orders and regulations affecting marketing (see www.asa.org.uk or www.cap.org.uk for a non-exhaustive list). The ASA maintains a rapport with those responsible for initiating or administering any laws that have a bearing on marketing communications. The system is reinforced by the legal backup provided for the work of the ASA by the Control of Misleading Advertisements Regulations 1988 (as amended) (see 61.10 below).

60.24   The Code, and the self-regulatory framework that exists to administer it, was designed and has been developed to work within and to complement these legal controls. It provides an alternative, and in some instances the only, means of resolving disputes about marketing communications. It also stimulates the adoption of high standards of practice in areas such as taste and decency that are extremely difficult to judge in law but that fundamentally affect consumer confidence in marketing communications.

60.25 There are also some important spheres that are governed by legislation enforced by local authority trading standards and environmental health officers. These include product packaging (except for on-pack promotions), weights and measures, statements on displays at point of sale and the safety of products.

60.26 Many Government agencies administer consumer protection legislation that ranges far wider and deeper than could be enforced through self-regulatory codes of practice. Marketers who break the law risk criminal prosecution or civil action. The Code requires marketers to ensure that all their marketing communications are legal, but the ASA is not a law enforcement body. Any matter that principally concerns a legal dispute will normally need to be resolved through law enforcement agencies or the Courts.

Media prerogative

60.27 The fact that a marketing communication conforms to the Code does not guarantee that every publisher will accept it. Media owners can refuse space to marketing communications that break the Code and they are also under no obligation to publish every marketing communication offered to them.

Investigations

(see ASA Complaints Procedure leaflet)

60.28 Complaints are investigated free of charge. They must be made in writing, within three months of the marketing communication's appearance (in exceptional circumstances, complaints about older marketing communications will be considered) and should be accompanied by a copy of the marketing communication or a note of where and when it appeared. The ASA may add challenges to those made by complainants and, as part of its routine research and monitoring, may also identify, investigate and publish results of its independent actions.

60.29 The identities of individual members of the public who complain are neither published nor revealed by the ASA to marketers without the complainants' express permission. Only the Courts or officials acting within their legal powers can compel the ASA to disclose to them information received in confidence. The identities of groups and of industry complainants such as competitors are disclosed and they must agree to the publication of their identities before their complaints can be pursued.

60.30 Equal weight is given to the investigation of all complaints irrespective of their source but the likely impact on, and consequent response of, those who may see the marketing communication will be taken into account. The Code requires industry complainants, wherever possible, to endeavour to resolve their differences between themselves or through their trade or professional organisations. To deter tit-for-tat disagreements, competitor complainants may be required to justify their complaints to the ASA.

60.31 Members of the public who complain may be asked by the ASA for a formal, written assurance that they have no commercial or other interest in registering a complaint. If they do have an interest, this will be disclosed to the marketer and will normally be included in the ASA's published ruling.

60.32 Complaints are not normally pursued if the point at issue is the subject of simultaneous legal action. In certain cases it may be more appropriate for an investigation to be undertaken by other consumer protection bodies. If so, the ASA will provide information or will try to redirect the complainant to the most appropriate qualified source of assistance.

60.33 Complaints generally fall into four broad categories: those that concern matters outside the scope of the Code; those where the complainant's interpretation of either the marketing communication or the Code does not correspond with that of the ASA (in some cases, these decisions are taken by the ASA Council); those that indicate that the marketer needs to make some modification that can be dealt with informally; and those that make out a case for a formal investigation. If the Council has previously ruled on the same or a similar marketing communication the complainant is notified of its judgment. Typical deadlines for responding to ASA investigations are available on www.asa.org.uk.

60.34 The Executive conducts an investigation into those complaints that are pursued; most are dealt with within six to 12 weeks (depending on the complexity of the matter), some are fast-tracked and completed within as little as 48 hours and others are given priority. Where necessary, the Executive takes advice from external expert consultants before producing a recommendation based on its findings for the ASA Council. Recommendations made by the Executive can, at its own request or the request of those affected, be considered by a CAP Panel. The Council will take into account the Panel's opinions. The final decision on complaints and on interpretation of the Code rests with the Council. Each week on www.asa.org.uk, the ASA publishes its adjudications on formally investigated complaints and a summary of complaints resolved informally and of those involving fulfilment, refund and database concerns.

60.35 The Executive is authorised by the Council and CAP to take interim action to ensure that marketing communications that break the Code are amended or withdrawn if it appears necessary to avoid further harm.

60.36 Members of the Executive are normally willing to discuss complaints with anyone directly involved subject to the obligations of confidentiality (see cl 2.7 above). The ASA may send confidential evidence to its external consultants, who are obliged not to disclose it to anyone else; the names of the ASA's consultants are available from the Executive to those directly involved. The ASA Council's adjudications on complaints may be circulated to interested parties, including the media.

60.37 The Code requires marketers to produce documentary evidence to substantiate their claims. All evidence submitted by marketers must be in English. No provision is made for oral hearings.

The Independent Review procedure

60.38 In exceptional circumstances, the ASA Council can be asked to reconsider its adjudication (including a Council decision not to investigate a complaint).

Requests for a review should contain a full statement of the grounds, be in writing and be addressed to the Independent Reviewer of ASA Adjudications, 5th Floor, 21 Berners Street, London, W1T 3LP. They should be sent within 21 days of the date on the ASA's letter of notification of an adjudication. The Independent Reviewer may waive this 21-day time limit if he judges it fair and reasonable to do so. Requests should come only from the complainant(s) or marketer. Those from the marketer or from an industry complainant should be signed by the Chairman, Chief Executive or equivalent;

requests made only by their solicitor or agency will not be accepted. All dealings with the Independent Reviewer must be in writing.

There are two grounds on which such a request can be made:

(1) Where additional relevant evidence becomes available (an explanation of why it was not submitted previously, in accordance with cl 3.1, will be required).

(2) Where there is a substantial flaw in the Council's adjudication or in the process by which that adjudication was made.

No review will proceed if the point at issue is the subject of simultaneous or contemplated legal action between anyone directly involved. Requests for review should make plain that no such action is underway or is contemplated.

The ASA will not delay publication of the relevant adjudication pending the outcome of a review save in exceptional circumstances (on the authorisation of the ASA Director General).

The Independent Reviewer will evaluate the substance of the request with advice from two Assessors (apart from requests about a Council decision not to investigate a complaint). The two Assessors are the Chairman of ASBOF (or nominee) and the Chairman of the ASA.

If the Independent Reviewer decides not to accept the request (in whole or in part) because he considers that it does not meet either of the two grounds set out above he will inform the person making the request accordingly.

If he decides to accept the request (in whole or in part) he will undertake, either by himself or with assistance from the ASA Executive or any other source of help or advice, such further investigation as he thinks appropriate. He will also inform the other parties to the case that a request for review has been accepted and will invite their comments on the submission made by the party requesting the review. At the conclusion of his investigation, he will make a recommendation to the ASA Council.

The Council's adjudication on reviewed cases is final.

The Independent Reviewer will inform all parties of the Council's decision.

Adjudications that are revised following a review will be published on www.asa.org.uk.

Europe

60.39 All member states of the European Union, and many non-EU European countries, have SROs that are broadly similar to the system in the UK. Together with organisations representing the advertising industry in Europe, those SROs are members of the European Advertising Standards Alliance (EASA), the single voice of the advertising industry in Europe on advertising self-regulation. The ASA is a founder member of EASA.

EASA is located in Brussels and meets regularly to co-ordinate the promotion and development of self-regulation at a European level.

Among its wide range of operations, EASA acts as a focal point for crossborder complaints investigated by individual members; consumers need complain only to the SRO in their country, no matter where the marketing communication originated.

EASA has published a statement of common principles, the core values that underpin each of its constituent SROs, and recommended standards for operating best practice in self-regulation that all SROs should seek to achieve.

Both are available on www.easa-alliance.org.

EASA is a source of information and research on self-regulation. It also helps in the development and establishment of SROs in Europe and corresponds internationally.

Additional information on the EASA's objectives, activities and publications, including the *Alliance Update* and order forms for *The Blue Book* containing an analysis of self-regulation in 22 European countries, is available from the EASA website on www.easa-alliance.org.

Sanctions

Introduction

61.1 The compliance figures published from time to time by the ASA have demonstrated that the vast majority of marketing communications comply with the Code. By providing advice, guidance and, in some cases, pressure, media owners, agencies and other intermediaries play a crucial role in ensuring compliance. If marketing communications break the Code, the marketers responsible are told by the ASA to amend or withdraw them. Most willingly undertake to do so. If they do not, sanctions are applied.

61.2   The ASA and CAP do not adopt a legalistic attitude towards sanctions and they ensure that sanctions are proportionate to the nature of the breach. They are, however, effective in the vast majority of cases. They focus on ensuring that non-compliant marketing communications are amended, withdrawn or stopped as quickly as possible.

61.3   The ASA and CAP are not restricted to applying sanctions only against marketers who have been subject to a formal investigation. If marketing communications are obviously misleading or offensive, the ASA and CAP may take compliance action in the absence of complaints or while an investigation proceeds (see 60.18 and 60.35).

Adverse publicity

61.4   Publicising the ASA's rulings is essential to sustaining wide acceptance of the system's integrity and the principle sanction available to the ASA is the unwelcome publicity that may result from the rulings it publishes weekly on www.asa.org.uk. Adverse publicity is damaging to most marketers and serves to warn the public. Anyone who is interested can access ASA rulings quicklyand easily on the website and can set up a profile-specific account so they are automatically notified by e-mail of relevant rulings as soon as they are published. ASA rulings receive a substantial amount of media coverage in international, national, regional and local newspapers, magazines and specialist journals, on national and regional TV and on national and local radio.

61.5   An adverse ASA ruling may have consequences for compliance with other codes or legal requirements. For example, personal data gathered as a result of a misleading marketing communication might not comply with the fair processing requirement in the first data protection principle of the Data Protection Act 1998.

Ad Alerts

61.6   CAP may issue Ad Alerts to its members, including the media, advising them to withhold their services from non-compliant marketers or deny the latter access to advertising space. Ad Alerts are issued at short notice, are carefully targeted for greatest impact, are sent electronically and, once issued, are available on a secure section of www.cap.org.uk to those who may need to consult them.

They contain the name and contact details of the non-compliant marketer, a description of the compliance problem and, if possible, a scanned image of the marketing communication in question.

Trading privileges and recognition

61.7 Many CAP trade associations and professional bodies offer their members, and others, recognition and trading privileges. They may revoke, withdraw or temporarily withhold those. For example, agency recognition offered by the print media members of CAP may be withdrawn or the substantial direct mail discounts offered by the Royal Mail on bulk mailings withheld. In exceptional cases of non-compliance, CAP members may expel companies from membership.

Pre-publication vetting

61.8 The ASA and CAP may require persistent offenders to have some or all of their marketing communications vetted by the CAP Copy Advice team until the ASA and CAP are satisfied that future communications will comply with the Code.

61.9 The poster industry members of CAP operate a poster pre-vetting sanction to deter abuse of the medium. If the ASA rules against a poster on the grounds of serious or widespread offence or social irresponsibility, the poster advertiser becomes a candidate for mandatory pre-vetting. If the poster industry members of CAP and the CAP Executive believe that the advertiser either is incapable of complying with the Code or seems to have deliberately flouted the Code with the intention of generating complaints, PR and subsequent notoriety, they will compel the advertiser to check future posters with the CAP Copy Advice team for a fixed period (usually two years).

Legal backstop

61.10 The ASA/CAP system is recognised by the Government, the Office of Fair Trading (OFT) and the Courts as one of the 'established means' of consumer protection in non-broadcast marketing communications. Under the Control of Misleading Advertisements Regulations

1988 (as amended), if a misleading marketing communication, or one containing an impermissible comparison, continues to appear after the Council has ruled against it, the ASA can refer the matter to the OFT. The OFT can seek an undertaking that it will be stopped from anyone responsible for commissioning, preparing or disseminating it. If that is not given or is not honoured, the OFT can seek an injunction from the Court to prevent its further appearance. Anyone not complying can be found to be in contempt of court and is liable to be penalised accordingly.

61.11   The ASA and CAP maintain a rapport with the OFT and with other bodies that have a responsibility for creating, administering or enforcing laws that have a bearing on marketing communications. If necessary, they may notify those bodies of non-compliant marketers and work with them to ensure that unacceptable marketing communications are amended, withdrawn or stopped.

61.12   The OFT and other 'qualified entities', such as Trading Standards Authorities, can use the Stop Now Orders (EC Directive) Regulations 2001 to enforce several existing consumer laws, including the Control of Misleading Advertisements Regulations 1988 (as amended). The ASA has agreed Case Handling Principles with the OFT to ensure that the Stop Now Orders bring about consumer protection without undermining the 'established means'.

Cross-border marketing communications

61.13   The Code does not apply to marketing communications in foreign media. If marketing communications appear in media based in countries that have selfregulatory organisations (SROs) that are members of EASA or if direct marketing originates from countries that have SROs that are members of EASA, EASA will co-ordinate cross-border complaints so the SRO in the country of origin of the marketing communication has jurisdiction; consumers need complain only to their SRO. If not, the ASA will take what action it can.

The SROs with jurisdiction will be formally responsible for applying any sanctions, though the ASA and CAP will, whenever they can, adopt a pragmatic approach to ensure that consumers are protected.

61.14   The ASA and CAP work increasingly closely with CAP trade associations and professional bodies, Trading Standards officers, Government departments, the OFT and other UK regulators, EASA and overseas SROs and statutory authorities to stop unacceptable marketing communications, particularly misleading and offensive mailings sent direct to UK consumers from overseas.

That work has achieved some success, but the ASA, CAP and other authorities, whether statutory or self-regulatory, experience particular difficulties in enforcing the Code and laws against companies based overseas. The Stop Now Orders referred to above, however, empower 'qualified entities' to take action to ensure compliance with the Control of Misleading Advertisements Regulations 1988 (as amended) throughout the European Union.

61.15   To clarify what can and cannot be done, the ASA and CAP have produced a fact sheet, 'Overseas Mailings', to explain how they tackle unacceptable mailings that originate outside the United Kingdom and to warn consumers to treat thosemailings with the utmost caution. That fact sheet is available on www.cap.org.uk.

History of self-regulation

Self-regulation is nothing new. Medieval guilds practiced self-regulation in that they inspected markets and measures, judged the quality of merchandise and laid down rules for their trade. In advertising and marketing, self-regulation can be traced back to the poster industry in the 1880s. The first Code of advertising was launched in 1925 by the Association of Publicity Clubs. And systematic scrutiny of advertising claims operated from 1926, when the newly established Advertising Association set up an advertising investigation department to 'investigate abuses in advertising and to take remedial action'.

In 1937, the International Chamber of Commerce developed an international code of advertising practice, the first of several international marketing codes which have provided a benchmark for many national systems of self-regulation.

The CAP (or the Code of Advertising Practice Committee, as it then was) came into existence in 1961 and was responsible for the first British Code of Advertising Practice and all subsequent Codes including this one. The Code covered all nonbroadcast advertising and in 1962 an independent body, the ASA, was established to administer it.

In 1974, a new improved funding mechanism for self-regulation was introduced in the form of the ASBOF. The new system brought an automatic levy of 0.1 per cent on all display advertising to fund the system. With it came an increased emphasis on public awareness of self-regulation and increased staffing to facilitate pre-vetting and monitoring.

Also in 1974, the first Code of Sales Promotion Practice was agreed, a recognition of the need to expand the role of the system to encompass promotional marketing.

Since 1962, advertising self-regulation has grown in stature. It now has all-party support and enjoys a widespread acceptance of its role in the protection of consumers. This acceptance led to the 1984 European Directive on Misleading Advertising being implemented in such a way as to allow the ASA to remain the principal regulator for misleading advertising in non-broadcast media, but with statutory reinforcement through the OFT.

Today, the system covers non-broadcast advertising, sales promotion and many aspects of direct marketing. It is supported by a range of other self-regulatory initiatives, including the various preference services run by the DMA, The Quality Standard for Mail Production and its recognition system and admark, a safe harbour scheme covering advertising on the Internet.

Yet the purpose of self-regulation remains as it was in the beginning: to maintain, in the best and most flexible way possible, the integrity of marketing communications in the interests of both the consumer and the trade.

CODE OF PRACTICE FOR TRADERS ON PRICE INDICATIONS

Published by, and reproduced here with the permission of, the Department of Trade and Industry.
October 2005

The DTI drives our ambition of 'prosperity for all' by working to create the best environment for business success in the United Kingdom. We help people and companies become more productive by promoting enterprise, innovation and creativity.

We champion UK business at home and abroad. We invest heavily in world-class science and technology. We protect the rights of working people and consumers. And we stand up for fair and open markets in the United Kingdom, Europe and the world.

Contents

Introduction

The Consumer Protection Act

1.   Section 20 of the Consumer Protection Act 1987 makes it a criminal offence for a person in the course of his business to give consumers a misleading price indication about goods, services, accommodation (including the sale of new homes) or facilities. It applies however you give the price indication—for example, in a TV or press advertisement, on a website, by e-mail or text message, in a catalogue or leaflet, on notices, price tickets or shelf-edge marking in stores, or if you give it orally, for example, on the telephone. The term 'price indication' includes price comparisons as well as indications of a single price.

2.   This Code of Practice is approved under s 25 of the Act, which gives the Secretary of State power to approve codes of practice to give practical guidance to traders. It is addressed to traders and sets out what is good practice to follow in giving price indications in a wide range of different circumstances, so as to avoid giving misleading price indications. The Code is not comprehensive. It cannot address every circumstance in which a misleading price may be given, particularly for new and innovative selling practices. It is guidance, rather than mandatory, although it may be taken into account in establishing whether an offence has been committed under the Act. You may, therefore, still give price indications which do not accord with this Code, provided they are not misleading. Equally, compliance with specific aspects of the Code will not, of itself, establish that a price indication is not misleading. Where an offence of giving a misleading price indication is alleged, a Court would have regard to all the relevant circumstances.

3.   'Misleading' is defined in s 21 of the Act. The definition covers indications about any conditions attached to a price, for example, additional charges that may be payable, about what you expect to happen to a price in future and what you say in price comparisons, as well as indications about the actual price the consumer will have to pay, for example, about a price which is additionally subject to VAT. It applies in the same way to any indications you give about the way in which a price will be calculated and to any relevant omissions from an indication which makes a price misleading.

Price comparisons

4. If you want to make price comparisons, you should do so only if you can justify them. You should be able to show that any claims you make are accurate and valid. As a general rule, you should only compare like with like, but comparisons with prices which you can show are being charged for very similar goods, services, accommodation or facilities and have applied for a reasonable period are also unlikely to be misleading. Guidance on these matters is contained in this Code.

Enforcement

5. Enforcement of the Consumer Protection Act 1987 is the responsibility of officers of the local weights and measures authority—usually called *Trading Standards Officers*. Trading Standards Officers operate in accordance with the Home Authority principle (under which a specific Trading Standards Service acts as the Home Authority for a major retailer with multi-store outlets) and with the principles of consultation and co-operation that are set out in the Enforcement Concordat. Further information about the Home Authority principle and the Enforcement Concordat can be obtained from your local Trading Standards Service or your Home Authority. Details of the location of your local Trading Standards Services can be obtained at the main Trading Standards website—http://www.tradingstandards.gov.uk. In Northern Ireland enforcement is the responsibility of the Department of Enterprise, Trade and Investment.

6. If a Trading Standards Officer has reasonable grounds to suspect that you have given a misleading price indication, the Act gives the Officer power to require you to produce any records relating to your business and to seize and detain goods or records which the Officer has reasonable grounds for believing may be required as evidence in court proceedings. Be prepared to cooperate with Trading Standards Officers and respond to reasonable requests for information and assistance. It is in your interest to be able to demonstrate that any claims you have made are accurate and valid. The Act makes it an offence to obstruct a Trading Standards Officer intentionally or to fail (without good cause) to give any assistance or information the Officer may reasonably require to carry out his duties under the Act.

Court proceedings

7. If you are taken to court for giving a misleading price indication, the court can take into account whether or not you have followed this Code. If you have done as the Code advises, that will not be an absolute defence but it will tend to show that you have not committed an offence. Similarly if you have done something the Code advises against doing it may tend to show that the price indication was misleading. If you do something that is not covered by the Code, your price indication will need to be judged only against the terms of the general offence. The Act provides for a defence of due diligence, that is, that you have taken all reasonable steps to avoid committing the offence of giving a misleading price indication, but failure to follow the Code of Practice may make it difficult to show this. The Act also provides for specific defences (eg, if a misleading price indication is given in a book, newspaper or magazine, film or broadcast programme, it is a defence for the publisher to show that the indication was not contained in an advertisement).

Regulations

8. The Act also provides power to make regulations about price indications and you should ensure that your price indications comply with any such regulations. There are specific regulations dealing with indications of exchange rates in Bureaux de Change[1], with price indications where different prices are charged depending on the method of payment (eg, by cash or credit card)[2] and with the resale of tickets for admission to places of entertainment[3]. Your local Trading Standards Service or Home Authority will be able to advise you on these regulations.

Other legislation

9. This Code deals only with the requirements of Pt III of the Consumer Protection Act 1987. In some areas there is other relevant legislation. For example, the way in which prices for goods sold by traders to consumers must be displayed is subject to regulations made under the Prices Act 1974 (eg, the Price Marking Order 2004[4]) and price indications about credit terms must comply with the Consumer Credit Act 1974 and the regulations made

[1] The Price Indications (Bureaux de Change) (No 2) Regulations SI 1992/737
[2] The Price Indications (Method of Payment) Regulations SI 1991/199
[3] The Price Indications (Resale of Tickets) Regulations SI 1994/3248
[4] SI 2004/102

under it. Those selling by distance contracts should also be aware of the requirements of the Consumer Protection (Distance Selling) Regulations 2000[5] and where traders make use of advertisements they should have regard to the relevant rules governing misleading advertising (further information on these is available from the Advertising Standards Association—www.asa.org.uk).

10. Your local Trading Standards Service, or your Home Authority will be pleased to advise you or direct you to sources of information on the regulations that are applicable to your particular business. Some legislation may also be accessed at the website of the Office of Public Sector Information—*http://www.legislation.opsi.gov.uk*

Definitions

Words and expressions used in the Code are explained below. However, the legal effect of terms used in the Consumer Protection Act 1987 and other legislation depends on the definitions in that legislation.

Accommodation	includes hotel and other holiday accommodation and new homes for sale freehold or on a lease of over 21 years but does not include rented homes.
Consumer	means anyone who might want the goods, services, accommodation or facilities, other than for business use.
Distance contract	means any contract concerning products concluded between a trader and a consumer by any means, without the simultaneous physical presence of the trader and the consumer.
Price	means the total amount the consumer will have to pay to get the goods, services, accommodation or facilities or any method which has been or will be used to calculate that amount.
Price comparison	means any indication given to consumers that the price at which something is offered to consumers is less than or equal to some other price.

---

[5] SI 2000/2334

Product	means goods, services, accommodation and facilities (but not credit facilities, except where otherwise specified).
Services and facilities	means any services or facilities whatever (including credit, banking and insurance services, purchase or sale of foreign currency, supply of electricity, and off-street car parking), making arrangements for a person to keep a caravan on land (unless the caravan is the person's main home) but not services provided by an employee to his employer under an employment contract.
Outlet	means any shop, store, stall or other place (including a vehicle or the consumer's home) and any means through which a distance contract may be concluded (including a website) at which goods, services, accommodation or facilities are offered to consumers.
Trader	means anyone (retailer, manufacturer, agent, service provider or other) who is acting in the course of a business.

Part 1: Price comparisons

1.1   Price comparisons generally

1.1.1   Information on different kinds of price comparisons is given in the paragraphs below, although it is the provisions of the Consumer Protection Act 1987 relating to misleading price indications with which you will ultimately need to comply. Generally, you should compare like with like and where a reduced price is claimed then the product should have been offered for sale at the higher price for at least 28 days in the previous six months in the same outlet. If your comparison does not meet those criteria then you should provide an explanation which is unambiguous, easily identifiable and (except where it is impractical, for instance, in distance contracts that are concluded orally) clearly legible to the consumer.

1.1.2   Always make the meaning of price indications clear. Do not leave consumers to guess whether or not a price comparison is being made. If no price comparison is intended, do not use words or phrases which, in their normal, everyday use and in the context in which they are used, are likely to give your customers the impression that a price comparison is being made. Price comparisons should always state the higher price as well as the price you intend to charge for the product (goods, services, accommodation or facilities). Do not make statements like 'sale price £5' or 'reduced to £39' without quoting the higher price to which they refer. If you refer to the previous price for the purpose of claiming there has been a reduction it should be to the cash price. If it is not, then an unambiguous, easily identifiable and clearly legible explanation of what the previous price referred to should be given.

1.1.3 It should be clear what sort of price the higher price is. For example, comparisons with something described by words like 'regular price', 'usual price' or 'normal price' should say whose regular, usual or normal price it is (eg, 'our normal price'). Descriptions like 'reduced from' and crossed out higher prices should be used only if they refer to your own previous price. Words should not be used in price indications other than with their normal everyday meanings.

1.1.4 Do not use initials or abbreviations to describe the higher price in a comparison, except for the initials 'RRP' to describe a recommended retail price or the abbreviation 'man. rec. price' to describe a manufacturer's recommended price (see paragraph 1.6.2).

1.1.5 Follow the part of the Code (ss 1.2 to 1.6 as appropriate) which applies to the type of comparison you intend to make.

1.2 Comparisons with the trader's own previous price

General

1.2.1 In any comparison between your present selling price and the last selling price at which the product was offered, you should state the previous price as well as the new lower price.

1.2.2 In any comparison with your own previous price:

(a) the previous price should be the last price at which the product was available to consumers in the previous six months unless the situation covered by paragraph 1.2.8 below applies;

(b) the product should have been available to consumers at that price for at least 28 consecutive days in the previous six months; and

(c)   the previous price should have applied (as above) for that period at the **same** outlet where the reduced price is now being offered.

The 28 days at (b) above may include public holidays, Sundays or other days of religious observance when the outlet was closed (or otherwise unavailable for business); and up to 4 days when, for reasons beyond your control, the product was not available for supply. The product must not have been offered at a different price between that 28-day period and the day when the reduced price is first offered.

1.2.3   If the previous price in a comparison does not meet one or more of the conditions set out in paragraph 1.2.2 above then:

(a)   the comparison should be fair and meaningful;

(b)   give a clear and positive explanation of the period for which and the circumstances in which that higher price applied. The explanation should be unambiguous, easily identifiable and clearly legible to the consumer.

For example, 'these goods were on sale here at the higher price from 1 February to 26 February' or 'these goods were on sale at the higher price in 10 or our 95 stores'. **Display the explanation clearly, and as prominently as the price indication.** You should not use general disclaimers saying for example that the higher prices used in comparison have not necessarily applied for 28 consecutive days.

1.2.4   A previous price used as a basis of a price comparison should be a genuine retail price. It should be a price at which you offered the goods for sale in the reasonable expectation that they could be sold by you at the higher price. In any case where a sale price is compared to a price that is higher than the usual retail price in the particular outlet, that fact should be made clear.

Food, drink and perishable goods

1.2.5   For any food and drink you need not give a positive explanation if the previous price in a comparison has not applied for 28 consecutive days, provided it was the last price at which the goods were on sale in the previous six months and applied in the same outlet where the reduced price is now being offered. This also applies to non-food items, if they have a shelf-life of less than six weeks.

Distance contracts

1.2.6 Where products are sold only through distance contracts, any comparison with a previous price should be with your own last price. If you sell the same products for different prices in different types of outlets (eg, charging a different price in your High Street store compared to a direct sale from your website), the previous price should be the last price at which you offered the product at the outlet in relation to which the claim is made. You should also follow the guidance in paragraphs 1.2.2 (a) and (b). If your price comparison does not meet these conditions, you should follow the guidance in paragraph

Factory outlets

1.2.7 Retailers located in factory outlets sites (ie, sites where it is a condition of tenancy that a substantial majority of the goods must be sold at a discount), who have not sold the same goods at a higher price in the same store, may display an unambiguous, easily identifiable and clearly legible general notice stating that all (or a specified proportion) of goods have been bought in from elsewhere, which may include outlets outside the United Kingdom. Specific comparisons and reductions made for particular items must comply with the other relevant guidance in this Code of Practice and they must be verifiable in the event of a challenge by the local Trading Standards Service or Home Authority.

Making a series of reductions

1.2.8 If you advertise a price reduction and then want to reduce the price further during the same sale or special offer period, the intervening price (or prices) need not have applied for 28 days. In these circumstances unless you use a positive explanation (paragraph 1.2.3):

(a)   the highest price in the series must have applied for 28 consecutive days in the last six months at the same outlet;

(b)   you must show the highest price, the intervening price(s); and

(c)   the current selling price.

1.3   Introductory offers, after-sale or after-promotion prices

1.3.1   Do not call a promotion an introductory offer unless you intend to continue to offer the same product for sale at the same outlet after the offer period is over and to do so at a higher price.

1.3.2   Do not allow an offer to run on so long that it becomes misleading to describe it as an introductory or other special offer. What is a reasonable period will depend on the circumstances (but, depending on the shelf-life of the product, it is likely to be a matter of weeks, not months). An offer is unlikely to be misleading if you state the date the offer will end and keep to it. If you then extend the offer period, make it clear that you have done so.

Quoting a future price

1.3.3   If you indicate an after-sale or after-promotion price, do so only if you are certain that, subject only to circumstances beyond your control, you will continue to offer identical products at that price for at least 28 days in the 3 months after the end of the offer period or after the offer stocks run out.

1.3.4   If you decide to quote a future price, write what you mean in full. Do not use initials to describe it (eg 'ASP', 'APP'). The description should be clearly and prominently displayed, with the price indication.

1.4   Comparisons with prices related to different circumstances

1.4.1   Comparisons should be fair and reasonable. You should only compare like with like or very similar products in terms of quality, composition and description. If there is a difference, then an unambiguous, easily identifiable and clearly legible explanation of the difference(s) should also be provided. This section covers comparisons with prices:

(a)   for different quantities (eg '15p each, 4 for 50p');

(b)   for goods in a different condition (eg 'seconds £20, when perfect £30');

(c)   for a different availability (eg price £50, price when ordered specially £60');

(d)   for goods in a totally different state (eg 'price in kit form £50, price ready-assembled £70'); or

(e)   for special groups of people (eg 'senior citizens' price £2.50, others £5').

General

1.4.2   Do not make comparisons with prices related to different circumstances unless the product is available in the different quantity, conditions etc at the price you quote. Make clear to consumers the different circumstances which apply and show them prominently with the price indication. Do not use initials (eg 'RAP' for 'ready-assembled price') to describe the different circumstances, but write what you mean in full.

'When perfect' comparisons

1.4.3   If you do not have the perfect goods on sale in the same outlet:

(a)   follow s 1.2 if the 'when perfect' price is your own previous price for the goods;

(b)   follow s 1.5 if the 'when perfect' price is another trader's price; or

(c)   follow s 1.6 if the 'when perfect' price is one recommended by the manufacturer or supplier.

Goods in a different state

1.4.4   Only make comparisons with goods in a totally different state if:

(a)   a reasonable proportion (say a third by quantity) of your stock of those goods is readily available for sale to consumers in that different state (eg, ready assembled) at the quoted price and from the outlet where the price comparison is made; or

(b)   another trader is offering those goods in that state at the quoted price and you follow s 1.5.

The price of a collection of items should only be compared with the previous price of the same collection of items, unless any differences are explained in an unambiguous, easily identifiable and clearly legible way. For instance, do not compare the price of a complete fitted kitchen with the price of the items when sold separately, unless this difference is explained in an unambiguous, easily identifiable and clearly legible way.

Prices for special groups of people

1.4.5   If you want to compare different prices which you charge to different groups of people (eg one price for existing customers and another for new customers, or one price for people who are members of a named organisation (other than the trader) and another for those who are not), do not use words like 'our normal' or 'our regular' to describe the higher price, unless it applies to at least half your customers.

1.5   Comparisons with another trader's prices

1.5.1   Comparisons should not be misleading. Only compare your prices with another trader's price if:

(a)   you know that the other trader's price which you quote is accurate and up-to-date—if the comparison becomes misleading it should be removed as soon as is practicable;

(b)   you give the name of the other trader clearly and prominently, with the price comparison;

(c)   you identify the circumstance where the other trader's price applies; and

(d)   the other trader's price which you quote applies to the same product—or to substantially similar product and you state any differences clearly (see paragraph 1.4).

Comparisons should also be with prices of outlets in the same locality, unless it can be shown that it makes no difference because of a national pricing policy.

1.5.2   Do not make statements like 'if you can buy this product elsewhere for less, we will refund the difference' about your 'own brand' products which other traders do not stock, unless your offer will also apply to other traders' equivalent goods. If there are any conditions attached to the offer (eg it only applies to goods on sale in the same town or excluding Internet sales) you should show them clearly and prominently, with the statement.

1.5.3 'Lowest price' claims must be backed up by suitable evidence to show that the trader is offering a lower price than competitors. Offering a 'price promise', for example, to beat a competitors' cheaper price if informed of that price by a customer, does not, of itself, justify a 'lowest price' claim if the latter cannot be supported. You should make clear that the claim is limited to a price matching promise if that is the case.

1.6 Comparisons with 'Recommended Retail Price' or similar

General

1.6.1 This Section covers comparisons with recommended retail prices, manufacturers' recommended prices, suggested retail prices, suppliers' suggested retail prices and similar descriptions. It also covers prices given to co-operative and voluntary group organisations by their wholesalers or headquarters organisations.

1.6.2 Do not use initials or abbreviations to describe the higher price in a comparison unless:

(a) you use the initials 'RRP' to describe a recommended retail price; or

(b) you use the abbreviation 'man. rec. price' to describe a manufacturer's recommended price.

Write all other descriptions out in full and show them clearly and prominently with the price indication.

1.6.3 Do not use a recommended price in a comparison unless:

(a) you can show that it has been recommended to you by the manufacturer or supplier as a price at which the product might be sold to consumers;

(b) you deal with that manufacturer or supplier on normal commercial terms. (This will generally be the case for members of co-operative or voluntary group organisations in relation to their wholesalers or headquarters organisations); and

(c) the price is not significantly higher than prices at which the product is generally sold at the time you make that comparison.

Do not use an 'RRP' or similar for goods that only you supply.

1.7   Pre-printed prices

1.7.1   Make sure you pass on to consumers any reduction stated on the manufacturer's packaging (eg 'flash packs'such as '10p off RRP').

1.7.2   You are making a price comparison if goods have a clearly visible price already printed on the packaging which is higher than the price you will charge for them. Such pre-printed prices are, in effect, recommended prices (except for retailers' own label goods) and you should follow paragraphs 1.6.1 to 1.6.4. You need not state that the price is a recommended price.

1.8   References to value or worth

1.8.1   Do not compare your prices with an amount described only as 'worth' or 'value'.

1.8.2   Do not present general advertising slogans which refer to 'value' or 'worth' in a way which is likely to be seen by consumers as a price comparison.

1.9   Sales or special events

1.9.1   If you have bought in items especially for a sale, and you make this clear, you should not quote a higher price when indicating that they are special purchases. Otherwise, your price indications for individual items in the sale which are reduced should comply with s 1.1 of the Code and whichever of ss 1.2 to 1.6 applies to the type of comparison you are making.

1.9.2   If you just have a general notice saying, for example, that all products are at 'half marked price', the marked price on the individual items should be your own previous price and you should follow s 1.2 of the Code.

1.9.3   Do not use general notices saying, eg 'half price sale' or 'up to 50 per cent off'unless the maximum reduction quoted applies to at least 10per cent of the range of products on offer at the commencement of the sale.

1.10   Free offers

1.10.1   Make clear to consumers, at the time of the offer for sale, exactly what they will have to buy to get the 'free offer'. If any sort of direct payment is required (eg, postal or delivery charges) and is not referred to in the price indication, this may be misleading.

1.10.2 If you give any indication of the monetary value of the 'free offer', and that sum is not your own present price for the product, follow whichever of ss 1.2 to 1.6 covers the type of price it is.

1.10.3 If there are any conditions attached to the 'free offer', give at least the main points of those conditions with the price indication and make clear to consumers where, before they are committed to buy, they can get full details of the conditions.

1.10.4 Do not claim that an offer is free if:

(a) you have imposed additional charges that you would not normally make;

(b) you have inflated the price of any product the consumer must buy or the incidental charges (for example, postage or premium rate telephone charges) the consumer must pay to get the 'free offer'; or

(c) you will reduce the price to consumers who do not take it up.

Part 2: Actual price to consumer

2.1 Indicating two different prices

2.1.1 The Consumer Protection Act 1987 makes it an offence to indicate a price for goods or services which is lower than the one that actually applies. You should not therefore show one price in an advertisement, website, window display, shelf marking or on the item itself, and then charge a higher price at the point of sale or checkout. In addition, specific regulations apply to particular types of sales and ways of selling—for example, retail sales (including the Internet), sales of food and drink which involve service, distance contracts, resale of tickets, package travel, etc. Your local Trading Standards Services or Home Authority will be pleased to advise you on the current regulations that are relevant to your business and of any good practice guidance which is also relevant.

2.2   Incomplete information and non-optional extras

2.2.1   Make clear in your price indication the full price consumers will have to pay for the product. The consumer should always be fully aware of the total cost including (eg, postage, packing, delivery charges, insurance, etc.) before they commit themselves to the purchase. Some examples of how to provide this information in particular circumstances are set out below.

Limited availability of product

2.2.2   Where the price you are quoting for products only applies to a limited number of, say, orders, sizes or colours, you should make this clear in your price indication in an unambiguous, easily identifiable and clearly legible way (eg,'available in other colours or sizes at additional cost').

Prices relating to differing forms of products

2.2.3   If the price you are quoting for particular products does not apply to the products in the form in which they are displayed or advertised, say so clearly in your price indication. For example, advertisements for self-assembly furniture and the like should make it clear that the price refers to a kit of parts.

Postage, packing and delivery charges

2.2.4   If you sell by distance contract, make clear any additional charges for postage, packing or delivery, so that consumers are fully aware of them before they commit themselves to buy. Where you cannot determine these charges in advance, you must indicate clearly how they will be calculated (eg, 'Royal Mail rates apply'), or specify the place where the information is given.

2.2.5   If you sell goods from an outlet and offer a delivery service for certain items, make it clear whether there are any separate delivery charges (eg, for delivery outside a particular area) and what those charges are, before the consumer is committed to buying.

Pricing in different currencies

2.2.6   There are rules about what information must in certain circumstances be provided on exchange rates and commission charges if you accept payment in a foreign currency in addition to sterling, and your local Trading Standards Service can advise you on them. There is a risk that your price indications could be considered misleading if you offer products that are dual priced with sterling and a foreign currency but you will only accept sterling and the sterling price is higher. In these circumstances you should make it clear that you only accept sterling, for instance by displaying a notice to that effect.

Valued Added Tax

(a)   Price indications to consumers

2.2.7   All price indications you give to private consumers, by whatever means, should include VAT.

(b)   Price indications to business customers

2.2.8   Prices may be indicated exclusive of VAT at an outlet or through advertisements from which most of your business is with business customers. If you also conduct business at that outlet or through these advertisements with consumers, however, you should make clear that the prices exclude VAT and you should:

(i)   display VAT inclusive prices with equal prominence, or;

(ii)   display prominent statements that the quoted prices exclude VAT and state the appropriate rate. If should be noted that VAT inclusive prices for all goods offered by traders to consumers are required by the Price Marking Order 2004[6] (further information can be obtained from your local Trading Standards Service).

(c)   Professional fees 2.2.9 Where you indicate a price (including an estimate) for a professional fee, make clear what it covers. The price should generally include VAT. In cases where the fee is based on an as-yet-unknown sum of money (eg, the sale price of a house), either:

(a)   quote a fee which includes VAT; or

(b)   make it clear that in addition to your fee the consumer would have to pay VAT at the current rate (eg, 'fee of 1.5 per cent of purchase price, plus VAT at 17.5 per cent').

Make sure that whichever method you choose is used for both the estimate and final bill.

---

[6] SI 2004/102

(d)   Building work

2.2.10   In estimates for building work, either include VAT in the price indication or indicate with equal prominence the amount or rate of VAT payable in addition to your basic figure. If you give a separate amount for VAT, make it clear that if any provisional sums in estimates vary then the amount of VAT payable would also vary.

Service, cover and minimum charges in hotels, restaurants and similar establishments

2.2.11   Do not include suggested optional sums, whether for service or any other item, in the bill presented to the customer. If your customers in hotels, restaurants or similar places must pay a non-optional extra charge, for example, a 'service charge':

(a)   incorporate the charge within fully inclusive prices wherever practicable; and

(b)   display the fact clearly on any price list or priced menu, whether displayed inside or outside (eg, by using statements like 'all prices include service')

2.2.12   It may not be practical to include some non-optional extra charges in a quoted price; for instance, if you make a flat charge per person or per table in a restaurant (often referred to as a 'cover charge') or a minimum charge. In such cases the charge should be shown as prominently as other prices on any list or menu, whether displayed inside or outside. Your local Trading Standards Service or Home Authority can advise you further on the legislation relevant to price marking in bars, restaurants and similar outlets.

Holiday and travel prices

2.2.13   If you offer a variety of prices to give consumers a choice (eg, paying more or less for a holiday depending on the time of year or the standard of accommodation), make clear in your brochure or website, or in any other price indication what the basic price is and what it covers. Give details of any optional additional charges and what those charges cover, or of the place where this information can be found, clearly and close to the basic price.

2.2.14   Any non-optional extra charges which are for fixed amounts should be included in the basic price and not shown as additions, unless they are only payable by some consumers. In that case you should specify, near to the details of the basic price, either what the amounts are and the circumstances in which they are payable, or where in the brochure etc the information is given.

2.2.15 Details of non-optional extra charges which may vary, or details of where in the brochure etc the information is given, should be made clear to consumers near to the basic price.

2.2.16 If you reserve the right to increase prices after consumers have made their booking, state this clearly with all indications of prices, and include prominently in your brochure full information on the circumstances in which a surcharge is payable and how it is to be calculated. There are specific rules limiting rights to increase package holiday prices in the Package Travel, Package Holidays and Package Tours Regulations 1992[7]

Ticket prices

2.2.17 If you sell tickets, whether for sporting events, cinema, theatre etc and your prices are higher than the regular price that would be charged to the public at the box office, that is, higher than the 'face value', you must make clear in any price indication what the 'face value' of the ticket is as well as the actual price that will be charged. Your local Trading Standards Service or Home Authority can advise you further on the legislation relevant to resale of tickets.

Call-out charges

2.2.18 Free call out claims should be only be made when there will be no charge to the consumer unless remedial work is undertaken with their agreement.

2.2.19 If you make a minimum call-out charge or other flat-rate charge (eg, for plumbing, gas or electrical appliance repairs etc carried out in consumers' homes), ensure that the consumer is made aware of the charge and whether the actual price may be higher (eg, if work takes longer than a specific time) before being committed to using your services.

Credit facilities

2.2.20 Price indications about consumer credit should also comply with the Consumer Credit Act 1974 and the regulations made thereunder governing the form and content of advertisements.

---

[7] SI 1992/3288

Insurance

2.2.21   Where actual premium rates for a particular consumer or the availability of insurance cover depend on an individual assessment, this should be made clear when any indication of the premium or the method of determining it is given to consumers.

Part 3: Price indications which become misleading after they have been given

3.1   General

3.1.1   The Consumer Protection Act 1987 makes it an offence to give a price indication which, although correct at the time, becomes misleading after you have given it, if:

(a)   consumers could reasonably be expected still to be relying on it; and

(b)   you do not take reasonable steps to prevent them doing so.

Clearly it will not be necessary or even possible in many instances to inform all those who may have been given the misleading price indication. However, you should always make sure consumers are given the correct information before they are committed to buying a product and be prepared to cancel any transaction which a consumer has entered into on the basis of a price indication which has become misleading.

3.1.2   The following paragraphs set out what you should do in some particular circumstances

3.2   Newspaper and magazine advertisements

3.2.1   If the advertisement does not say otherwise, the price indication should apply for a reasonable period (as a general guide, at least seven days or until the next issue of the newspaper or magazine in which the advertisement was published, whichever is longer). If the price indication becomes misleading within this period make sure consumers are given the correct information before they are committed to buying the product.

3.3   Mail order advertisements, catalogues, leaflets, websites and similar advertising

3.3.1   Paragraph 3.2.1 above also applies to the time for which these price indications should be made. If a price indication becomes misleading within the period set out in paragraph 3.2.1, make the correct price indication clear to anyone who orders the product to which it relates. Do so before the consumer is committed to buying the product and, wherever practicable, before the goods are sent to the consumer.

3.4   Selling through agents

Holiday brochures and travel agents

3.4.1   Surcharges are covered in paragraph 2.2.16. If a price indication becomes misleading for any other reason, tour operators who sell direct to consumers should follow paragraph 3.3.1 above, and tour operators who sell through travel agents should follow paragraphs 3.4.2 and 3.4.3 below.

3.4.2   If a price indication becomes misleading while your brochure is still current, make this clear to the travel agents to whom you distributed the brochure. Be prepared to cancel any holiday bookings consumers have made on the basis of a misleading price indication.

3.4.3   In the circumstances set out in paragraph 3.4.2, travel agents should ensure that the correct price indication is made clear to consumers before they make a booking.

Insurance and independent intermediaries

3.4.4   Insurers who sell their products through agents or independent intermediaries should take all reasonable steps to ensure that all such agents who are known to hold information on the insurer's premium rates and terms of the cover provided are told clearly of any changes in those rates or terms.

3.4.5   Agents, independent intermediaries and providers of quotation systems should ensure that they act on changes notified to them by an insurer.

3.5   Changes in the rate of value added tax

3.5.1 If your price indications become misleading because of a change in the general rate of VAT, or other taxes paid at point of sale, make the correct price indication clear to any consumers who order products. Do so before the consumer is committed to buying the product and, wherever practicable, before the goods are sent to the consumer. For a period of 14 days from the date a VAT change takes effect, a general notice or notices may be used to indicate the adjustment necessary in prices to take account of the new VAT rate.

Part 4: Sale of new homes

4.1 A 'new home' is any building, or part of a building to be used only as a private dwelling which is either:

(a) a newly-built house or flat, or

(b) a newly-converted existing building which has not previously been used in that form as a private home.

4.2 The Consumer Protection Act 1987 and this Code apply to new homes which are either for sale freehold or on a long lease, ie, with more than 21 years to run. In this context the term 'trader' covers not only a business vendor, such as a developer, but also an estate agent acting on behalf of such a vendor. For provisions applicable to commercial property, or to residential property which is not a new home, you should consult your local Trading Standards Service or Home Authority.

4.3 You should follow the relevant provision of Pt 1 of the Code if:

(a)   you want to make a comparison between the price at which you offer new homes for sale and any other price; or

(b)   you offer an inclusive price for new homes which also covers such items as furnishings, domestic appliances and insurance and you compare their value with, for example, High Street prices for similar items.

4.4   Part 2 of the Code gives details of the provisions you should follow if:

(a)   the new houses you are selling, or any goods or services which apply to them, are only available in limited numbers or ranges;

(b)   the sale price you give does not apply to the houses as displayed; or

(c)   there are additional non-optional charges payable.

COUPONS–GUIDANCE NOTES

Published by, and reproduced here with the permission of, the Institute of Sales Promotion, Arena House, 66–68 Pentonville Road, Islington, London, N1 9HS. Tel: 020 7837 5340. Fax: 020 7837 5326. Website: http://www.isp.org.uk. E-mail: enquiries@isp.org.uk

Coupons—guidance notes

When a coupon is issued it is handled by distribution media, the public, retailers and clearing houses. Accordingly, it must be made clear to consumers what they are being offered, where the offer can

be redeemed and the time duration for the offer; retailers are relied upon to accept coupons and give consumers the correct saving and it is in the interest of all promoters to ensure that their coupons can be processed quickly and efficiently by both retailers and clearing houses.

Anyone responsible for the design and/or issue of a coupon that is intended to be redeemed through the retail or wholesale trade should refer to these Notes for Guidance to ensure that all coupons adhere to the basic requirements of good coupon design.

The design of a coupon—interactive!

Refer the following page for the Design of a Coupon.

Scope

(a) These Notes for Guidance cover the accepted basic requirements for a coupon which gives 'money off' a nominated product and which is designed to be redeemed through the retail or wholesale trade. They outline its design, size, redemption and handling requirements.

(b) They have been prepared jointly by e-centre UK, the British Retail Consortium, the Food and Drink Federation, the Institute of Sales Promotion and have been endorsed by the Federation of Wholesale Distributors and are accepted by these bodies as standard practice.

(c) Special uses of coupons, such as alternative value coupons and those requiring 'proof of purchase' to be attached, are more difficult to handle. Special conditions are likely to apply in relation to handling costs which need to be negotiated on an individual company basis during the planning of the promotion. These types of coupon are, however still subject to these Notes for Guidance.

Additional bar codes (EG, PIN/URN)

- Additional bar codes can be added to the coupon to provide more information for either the manufacturer, retailer or coupon

Bar code

Internal code
(if required)

0999 05362

`9 "912342"740203">`

COUPON
OFF NEXT
PURCHASE OF

VALID UNTIL DD.MM.YY

20P

Bloggo's

BAKED BEANS

240g ONLY

at

STORENAME

TO THE CUSTOMER
This coupon can be used as part
payment for (Brand/Product). Only one
coupon can be used against each item
purchased. Please do not attempt to
redeem the coupon against any other
product, as refusal to accept may cause
embarrassment and delay at the
checkout.

TO THE RETAILER
Bloggo Ltd will redeem this coupon at
its face value provided ONLY that it
has been taken in part payment for a
(Brand/Product) Bloggo Ltd reserve
the right to refuse payment. Against
misredeemed coupons. Please submit
coupons to Bloggo Ltd, Dept 123,
Town, County.

Product
details

Retailers

Instructions

Closing dates

Value

Size
and
shape

clearing house or all parties. This information is usually encoded in a PIN/URN bar code.

- For example, these can be printed using a Code 39 or an Interleaved 2 of 5 symbol. Contact your clearing house for further information, symbol content and advice. The scanning quality of these symbols should also be checked before circulation.

- This bar code should be printed where possible horizontal to the main bar code and at least 5 mm from the edge of the main bar code (including light margins) so as to avoid mis-scans. If the reverse of the coupon is used, the main bar code should be on the front of the coupon and the PIN/URN code on the reverse.

- This additional bar code can be placed anywhere on the coupon, ensuring that its placement will not impact the clarity of the coupon, eg, along the top left corner of the coupon. Contact your clearing house for guidance.

- The additional bar code can be used to track the promotion, tie the coupon back to information in a database or to identify specific information such as demographics etc.

Additional considerations for ON-PACK coupons

- Care should be taken to ensure that the coupon bar code and URN/PIN are not visible at the time of product purchase. This is to avoid potential confusion at the checkout.

- Promoters should ensure that coupons which are attached to labels or direct to packages are properly secured to prevent loss, yet remain detachable.

- Coupons should be situated so as not to become soiled or stained by either direct contact with, or use of, the product.

- Where coupons are embodied as part of a special pack and are to be redeemed against the next purchase, the words 'off next purchase' must appear in one bold typeface, size and colour.

- Careful consideration should be given as to the desirability of a closing date, especially where the product carries an extended 'minimum durability' date. In any event, the coupon closing date should always exceed the sell-by date of the product.

- When on-pack coupons coincide with any other kind of special on-pack price or money-off marking applied by the promoter, then one should be clearly differentiated from the other.

Allocation of coupon numbers to promotions

The structure of a coupon number is as follows:

Coupon Identifier (allocated by e-centre)	Issuer Number (allocated by e-centre)	Reference Number (sequential number allocated by the company responsible for coding the coupon)	Value (redemption value in pence, max. £9.98 = 998)	Check Digit (e-centre help page)
99	NNN	NNN	VVV	C

NB. Different coupon reference numbers must be allocated when:

i)   there is any change in the face value;

ii) there is any change in the expiry date;

iii) there is any change in the promotion;

NB. The Issuer number changes when the brand owner changes. All future coupons issued should use the new brand owners Issuer Numbers. Failure to do so could incur costs on both parties.

For values in excess of £9.98, 999 should be placed as the value in the bar code and the actual value should be printed on the coupon. Please notify your handling house in advance.

The following promotions CAN be encoded using a coupon:

- **Money-off next purchase.** This encodes a specific amount to be deducted off a specified product within a specified retailer. A single coupon can only encode one amount per product to be promoted.

- **Free Product Coupons.** Where there is an intention to provide consumers with a coupon for the entire purchase price of a product, special care is needed. Promoters wishing to issue 'free' product coupons are advised to consult their trade customers before issue. The coupon should clearly show a fixed value ie, 'Free up to a maximum retail price of £1.49' or Free up to a value of £1.49', which will be the amount redeemable irrespective of the Retail Price charged by the trader. This value can either be encoded in the bar code or '000' can be encoded as the coupon value to identify a free product coupon.

Certain promotions CANNOT be encoded using a coupon such as:

- Percentage off a product(s), money off on a variable weight item etc.

Trade notification

- Promoters should notify their trade customers in advance of their intention to issue on-pack coupons. It is also advisable to notify the trade in advance of major off-pack coupon campaigns.

- Outer cases containing coupon packs should be readily identified as such.

- During a "cross-couponing" campaign, promoters should, ensure that both brands are stocked by their trade customers

Materials

- Coupons should be printed on durable material of a weight and texture which is easy to handle without coupons sticking together or ripping. Materials such as polythene or cellophane are feasible although special care will be needed to ensure that the bar code will scan. The use of unusual materials for coupons should be discussed with both trade customers and the clearing house prior to production.

- Unusual or difficult materials, eg. foil, tub lids etc., can cause handling problems at the retailer or clearing house.

Coupons usage in non-printed matter

- For information and advice on Internet and electronic coupons please consult the ISP's Electronic Coupons paper.

- All coupon usage will be covered either by this paper or the Electronic Coupons paper.

Coupon handling costs

Where promotional schemes take the form of coupons redeemable through the trade you will incur the following costs:

- A trade handling allowance for the retail trade. This benchmark figure is agreed between the Food and Drink Federation and the British Retail Consortium.

- A handling charge and associated costs from your coupon clearing house. (These costs should be budgeted for when planning a campaign.)

Checklist

- Check that the promotion is suitable for the use of a money-off coupon.

- Ensure that the coupon wording is legal, unambiguous and clear for the customer to understand.

- Ensure that the coupon identifies the value, the product, promoter and relevant retailers, as detailed in this brochure.

- The coupon clearing house must be notified in advance if the additional information needs to be captured or the coupons need to be retained.

- Ensure the coupon number is correctly compiled and is encoded within the EAN-13 symbol.

- Check the size of the bar code symbol, both the magnification and the bar height.

- Ensure that there are adequate quiet zones for the bar code symbol.

- Ensure that key lines are not surrounding the bar code on the final coupon.

- Check that the contrast between the bars and the background is adequate and that the colours chosen will scan.

- Ensure that any additional PIN/URN bar codes have been correctly positioned and encode the correct information (see section headed Additional Bar Codes).

- For on-pack coupons, check the position of the coupon on the final product to ensure the coupon bar code cannot be scanned at the point of sale.

- Handling and clearing houses must be notified in advance of coupon campaigns, and additionally should be notified if the coupon is subject to over-redemption insurance cover.

- Ensure that no shrink-wrap, tape or other printing will obscure the bar code symbol on the finished product.

- If in doubt, seek guidance from your clearing or handling house.

Endorsed By:
e-centre
The British Retail Consortium
The Federation of Wholesale Distributors
The Food and Drink Federation

INSTITUTE OF SALES PROMOTION: GUIDELINES FOR BRIEFING FULFILMENT HOUSES

Published by, and reproduced here with the permission of, the Institute of Sales Promotion, Arena House, 66-68 Pentonville Road, Islington, London N1 9HS. Tel: 020 7837 5340. Fax: 020 7837 5326. Website: www.isp.org.uk. Email: enquiries@isp.org.uk

Promoter or agency brief

The following Checklist is information the Promoter/Agency needs to give the Handling House for briefing purposes.

NB

1. If all the details are not known then give clear assumptions on which the Fulfilment House can base costs, and remember that if these assumptions change, costs may also change.

2. There are potential benefits in involving a Fulfilment House as early as possible in the planning of a promotion. The House may be able to add value in terms of design or presentation from their experience.

(a) Title and brief description of the promotion:

- Start and close dates.

- Quantities involved (including contingency plans).

- Promotional media—on pack, direct mail, leaflet, sample site, door to door, Internet.

- Response rates—anticipated volume and pattern.

- Is the promotion insured? If so, what specific spec has been required by the insurer?

(b) Applications:

- Application form or plain paper? Send sample. Phone/Internet applications?

- Special instructions eg, one per household.

- Tolerance levels eg, POP's, cash contributions, 'one per household'.

- Payment: cash, cheque, credit card. Await cheque clearance before despatch?

- Proof of purchase tolerance levels.

- Storage of POP's: with application? In-bulk? Destroy?

    - If destroying—burn or recycle. Security issues?

- Data-capture: what?

    - Name, address, date of birth, e-mail address, tick boxes?
    - De-dupe by name? Address?
    - Separate opt-out database.
    - PIN number usage and recognition.
    - Is the data to be used for analysis or to add to an existing database?

- Rejection of Application—see (g) Consumer Queries.

(c) Postage/Carriage:

- Delivery speed eg, 1st or 2nd Class, Mailsort; Proof of Delivery required; Insurance required.

(d) Packing:

- Samples of ALL components for size/weight.

- Packing requirements.

- Packaging samples: who supplies?

- Additional Inserts eg, compliment slip.

(e) Banking:

- Paid into Promoters bank (supply details) or client account?

- If client account, how and when repaid?

- Postal Float; invoiced or deducted?

- Bounced cheques.

- Confirm whether banking charges to include cheque clearance.

(f) Stock:

- List of all stock required by the Fulfilment House eg, premiums, packaging, stationery. Send samples.

- Will these be sourced by the Promoter/Agency or by the Fulfilment House?

- Delivery Schedules; Supplier contact details; pallet or handball delivery?

- Reports on stock levels needed weekly/monthly?

- Will quality checks be required?

- Storage requirements eg, temperature control, sell-by dates, rotation.

- Plans for re-ordering and/or disposal at end of promotion.

- Insurance requirements.

(g) Consumer queries:

- Phone: is a dedicated line required?
    - Local, freephone, premium or standard rate.

- Written: stock letters? Promoter or Handling House letterheads?

- E-mail queries?

- Is the Promotion affected by the 'distance selling' regulations? If so are specific arrangements required?

(h) Account management:

- Reports, daily/weekly/monthly etc:
    - Format: fax, post, e-mail.
    - Information required: redemptions, volume, stock, customer services, banking.

- List authorised contacts at the Promoter and Agency (if applicable).

- Detail any requirements for regular meetings.

- See attached notes on relationship management.

(i) Promotion Data:

- Will a data file of respondents be required? If so when?

- Format required.

- Manipulation, eg, de-duping, adding mail-sort codes.

Note:

1. Seek advice on a suitable Fulfilment House. You need to assure yourself of their ability to handle your requirements and of their financial probity. Ask for a client's list and check credentials. Better still obtain a good recommendation.

2. Involve the Fulfilment House at the earliest possible stage. You should visit any house you seriously contemplate using to see the site, meet the people, look at storage facilities etc.

3. Many Promoters maintain an on-going relationship with one or two Houses with whom they have a contract that covers key working practices. This enables a new brief to concentrate on the specific variables.

Once you have your responses:

When comparing two or more competitive quotations extreme care needs to be taken to compare like with like. The clarity of your brief will help to ensure that the responses will be broken down in a way that enables comparisons to be made accurately. You may specifically ask for the response to be set out in a user-friendly of pre-specified way.

- Watch particularly for costs that are not specified, eg, monthly minimum cost, and ask for confirmation that there are none.

- Make sure that storage costs and stock handling costs are transparent and explained.

- Ensure that banking charges include cheque clearance charges.

Above all, if you are not sure, ask for clarification before you proceed—accept responsibility and do not make assumptions.

CHARTERED INSTITUTE OF PURCHASING & SUPPLY: PROFESSIONAL CODE OF ETHICS

Published by, and reproduced here with the permission of, the Chartered Institute of Purchasing and Supply, Easton House, Easton on the Hill, Stamford, Lincolnshire PE9 3NZ. Tel: 01780 756777. Fax: 01780 751610. Website: www.cips.org

An introduction to our Code of ethics

1. Members of our Institute undertake to work to exceed the expectations of the following Code and will regard the Code as the basis of best conduct in the Purchasing and Supply profession.

2. Members should seek the commitment of their employer to the Code and seek to achieve widespread acceptance of it amongst their fellow employees.

3. Members should raise any matter of concern of an ethical nature with their immediate supervisor or another senior colleague if appropriate, irrespective of whether it is explicitly addressed in the Code.

Key principles

4. Members shall always seek to uphold and enhance the standing of the Purchasing and Supply profession and will always act professionally and selflessly by:

(a)   Maintaining the highest possible standard of integrity in all business relationships, both inside and outside the organisations where they work.

(b)   Rejecting any business practice which might reasonably be deemed improper and never using their authority for personal gain.

(c)   Enhancing the proficiency and stature of the profession by acquiring and maintaining current technical knowledge and the highest standards of ethical behaviour.

(d)   Fostering the highest possible standards of professional competence amongst those for whom they are responsible.

(e)   Optimising the use of resources which they are responsible or influence to provide the maximum benefit to their employing organisation.

(f)   Complying both with the letter and the spirit of:

   (i)   The law of the country in which they practise.

   (ii)   Institute guidance on professional practice.

   (iii)   Contractual obligations.

5.   Members should never allow themselves to be deflected from these principles.

Guidance

6.   In applying these principles, members should follow the guidance set out below:

- Declaration of interest—any personal interest which may affect or be seen by others to affect a member's impartiality in any matter relevant to his or her duties should be declared.

- Confidentiality and accuracy of information—the confidentiality of information received in the course of duty should be respected and should never be used for personal gain. Information given in the course of duty should be honest and clear.

- Competition—the nature and length of contracts and business relationships with suppliers can vary according to circumstances. These should always be constructed to ensure deliverables and benefits. Arrangements which might in the long term prevent the effective operation of fair competition should be avoided.

- Business gifts—business gifts, other than items of very small intrinsic value such as business diaries or calendars, should not be accepted.

- Hospitality—the recipient should not allow him or herself to be influenced or be perceived by others to have been influenced in making a business decision as a consequence of accepting hospitality. The frequency and scale of hospitality accepted should be managed openly and with care and should not be greater than the member's employer is able to reciprocate.

Decisions and advice

7. When it is not easy to decide between what is and is not acceptable, advice should be sought from the member's supervisor, another senior colleague or the Institute as appropriate. Advice on any aspect of the Code is available from the Institute.

This Code was approved by the Council of CIPS on 16 October 1999

USEFUL CONTACTS

Advertising Standards Authority
Mid-City Place, 71 High Holborn, London, WC1V 7QT
Tel: 020 7492 2222
Fax: 020 7242 3696
Website: www.asa.org.uk

Advertising Standards Board of Finance Ltd
5th Floor, 21 Berners Street, London, W1T 3LP
Tel: 020 7580 7071
Fax: 020 7580 7057
Website: www.asbof.co.uk

Broadcast Advertising Standards Board of Finance Ltd,
5th Floor, 21 Berners Street, London, W1T 3LP
Tel: 020 7580 7071
Fax: 020 7580 7057
Website: www.basbof.co.uk

Broadcast Advertising Clearance Centre
2nd Floor, 4 Roger Street, London, WC1N 2JX
Tel: 0207 339 4700
Website: www.bacc.org.uk

Chartered Institute of Purchasing and Supply
Easton House, Easton on the Hill, Stamford, Lincs PE9 3NZ
Tel: 01780 756777
Fax: 01780 751610
Website: www.cips.org

Committee of Advertising Practice (CAP)
Mid-City Place, 71 High Holborn, London, WC1V 6QT
Tel: 020 7492 2222
Fax: 020 7404 3696
e-mail: enquiries@cap.org.uk
Website: www.cap.org.uk

Direct Marketing Association
DMA House, 70 Margaret Street, London, W1W 8SS
Tel: 020 7291 3300
Fax: 020 7323 4426
Website: www.dma.org.uk

European Advertising Standards Alliance
10a Rue de la Pépinière, B-1000 Brussels, Belgium
Tel: +32 (0)2 513 7806
Fax: +32 (0)2 513 2861
Website: www.easa-alliance.org

Independent Committee for the Supervision of Standards of Telephone Information Services
Clove Building, 4 Maguire Street, London, SE1 2NQ
Tel: 020 7940 7474
Fax: 020 7940 7456
Website: www.icstis.org.uk

Independent Reviewer of ASA Adjudications
5th Floor, 21 Berners Street, London, W1T 3LP

Information Commissioner's Office
Wycliffe House, Water Lane, Wilmslow, Cheshire, SK9 5AF
Information Line: 01625 545745;
Fax: 01625 524510
Website: www.ico.gov.uk

Institute of Sales Promotion
Arena House, 66–68 Pentonville Road, Islington, London, N1 9HS
Tel: 020 7837 5340
Fax: 020 7837 5326
Website: www.isp.org.uk

Office of Fair Trading
Fleetbank House, 2–6 Salisbury Square, London, EC4Y 8JX
Tel: 020 7211 8000
Fax: 020 7211 8800
Website: www.oft.gov.uk

Preference Services
DMA House, 70 Margaret Street, London, W1W 8SS

E-mail Preference Service
UK Address: Deltey House, Thornbridge Road, Iver Heath, Bucks,
SLO 0PU
Tel: 01895 850 181
Fax: 01895 850 383
Website: www.dmaconsumers.org.emps.html

Fax Preference Service
Tel: 020 7291 3330
Fax: 020 7323 4226
Website: www.fpsonline.org.uk

Mailing Preference Service
Tel: 020 7291 3310
Fax: 020 7323 4226
Website: www.mpsonline.org.uk

Telephone Preference Service
Tel: 020 7291 3320
Fax: 020 7323 4226
Website: www.tpsonline.org.uk

The Quality Standard for Mail Production (The QMP Register Ltd.)
P.O. Box 191, Cirencester, GL7 5WS
Tel: 01285 750511
e-mail: info@qmp.org.uk

Radio Advertising Clearance Centre
77 Shaftesbury Avenue, London W1D 5DU
Tel: 020 7306 2620
Fax: 020 7306 2645
Website: www.racc.co.uk

The Safe Home Ordering Protection Scheme (S.H.O.P.S.)
18a King Street, Maidenhead, SL6 1EF
Tel: 01628 641930
Fax: 01628 637112
e-mail: enquiries@shops-uk.org.uk

WebTrader UK Scheme—Centre for Secure Internet Trade,
18a King Street, Maidenhead, SL6 1EF
Tel: 01628 641936
Fax: 01628 637112
e-mail: admin@WebTraderUK.org.uk

INDEX

[all references are to page]